ESSENCE of an IDEALIST

by

JOHN P. ROACH JR.

authorHOUSE®

AuthorHouse™
1663 Liberty Drive
Bloomington, IN 47403
www.authorhouse.com
Phone: 1-800-839-8640

Published by AuthorHouse 11/13/2012

ISBN: 978-1-4772-6441-6 (sc)
ISBN: 978-1-4772-6442-3 (hc)
ISBN: 978-1-4772-6443-0 (e)

Library of Congress Control Number: 2012915695

Any people depicted in stock imagery provided by Thinkstock are models, and such images are being used for illustrative purposes only. Certain stock imagery © Thinkstock.

This book is printed on acid-free paper.

Because of the dynamic nature of the Internet, any web addresses or links contained in this book may have changed since publication and may no longer be valid. The views expressed in this work are solely those of the author and do not necessarily reflect the views of the publisher, and the publisher hereby disclaims any responsibility for them.

Editor, Sherri Lee Books
Architecture by John Patrick Roach Jr.
Front Cover: Idyllic setting: Yosemite National Park, CA
Back Cover: Deborah J. Johnson

Works of *John P. Roach Jr.*

HISTORICAL NOVELS
Mt. Soledad Love Story (Aristotle and Thomas Aquinas)
CALIFORNIA, The First 100 Years (Padre Serra to the Golden Spike)

BIOGRAPHICAL NOVELS
The Fourteenth State (Ethan Allen)
Triumph of the Swan (Richard Wagner and King Ludwig II of Bavaria)
Absinthe (Edgar Degas, A Leader in the Impressionist Revolution)
The Mighty Kuchka (Nikolai Rimsky-Korsakov and The Russian Five.)
Essence of an Idealist (The First of Five Volumes
of Autobiography of a Common Man.)

INSPIRATIONAL BOOKS
Serial Monogamy (A quest for Success, Happiness and Love)
Around the World in a Wheelchair (a
motivational book for the disabled)
Thanks for the Memories Cookbook (Deborah J. Johnson and Friends)

TRAVEL
Experience America's Finest City on the San Diego Trolley

SCIENCE FICTION
Inquiring Minds (Teens challenge education system)

WEBSITE www.JPRoach.org

contents

dedication
To the greatest gift of my life, my children.

preface

ESSENCE of an IDEALIST.

From the Latin word, esse, *to be.* To exist.

If we exist we have essence. When we exist we have choices to make from the very moment we recognize our own existence.

This book is about a person who chose to be an idealist, a person who set goals for himself at a very early age and achieved most of them by creativity, rather than money.

Do not think it is easy to be an idealist? Certainly not in my case, those around you continually remind you to be more practical and advise you, that your goals are neither realistic nor pragmatic.

Do idealists fail? Of course they do and some quit to blend in with everyone else. Others recognize their own failure, change direction and try again, and again until they succeed.

This book is true account of the author's quest to find his purpose in life. A quest that contains so many failures and so many successes that one questions the trials of an idealist.

We tend to categorize idealists as crazy Don Quixote types, charging at windmills to protect the chastity of his Dulcinea. When in fact, the true romantic recognizes, that both author, Cervantes and subject Don Quixote, appearing as an old chivalrous knight in rusty armor truly understood the power of love.

The idealist in this true story seeks adventure at a very early age and even though he finds it he never stops seeking more challenging adventures. The same is true for success. Success so often is measured in dollars as so aptly put in *Atlas Shrugged* by Ayn Rand.

By mid-life this author has become a millionaire and questions the materialistic rewards of success. He concludes that the accumulation of dollars and materialism are not the answer to happiness, for that which you own, owns you.

Should success then be re-defined.? Perhaps. Success could be defined as happiness and only the happiness, within you. If you are truly happy, you are successful.

This quest contains both successes and failures to find his purpose in life.

I'm writing this while maturing in age and knowledge, and if my life ends tomorrow it shall be said by my friends that I sought adventure, success, happiness and love and you can judge for yourself whether or not I found it.

chapter 1
BEING A KID!

I'M WRITING this while maturing in age and knowledge and if my life ends tomorrow it shall be said by my friends that I sought adventure, success, happiness and love and you can judge for yourself whether or not I found it.

John James and Mary (Molly) Roach and Family

Four brothers named Roche from County Cork Ireland, arriving together in the 1800s at Ellis Island immigration had their last name Americanized, from Roche to Roach. Once on land in New York City the Roach brothers sought employment wherever they could find it. Some settled, just across the Hudson River in Union City, NJ.

Hyacinth Roach made it all the way to California where the family lost track of him. Some speculate that he or his off-spring, may have become the Hal Roach Academy Award winning producer.

My Grandpa, John James Roach took the ferry to work in New York City each morning for a nickel. John James and Mary Roach brought up their daughter Marian and sons John and James. James died of the plague at age 12. So even in America times were not easy.

I was Born to a hard working middle class family in Union City NJ on August 13, 1936 and named after my father John Patrick Roach. Dad met my mother Alberta Huber an actress playing Ruth in the Passion Play in Union City, NJ where he played the violin in the orchestra. You can't choose your parents, but wow, I sure did get good ones.

Alberta Huber, actress.

My father was a page boy at age 19 on the floor of the New York Exchange on Black Tuesday during the October 29, Crash. He majored in accounting at Pace College in New York. His father John James Roach worked for the Post Office also across the Hudson River in New York City and suggested to his son, that with our country in a severe depression, that he find a secure government job with the Post Office.

Dad left the stock exchange and worked for the US Railway Post Office, sorting mail in a Railway car from New York City to Montréal as the train picked up and left off bags of mail hanging on posts between the two cities. He was frugal and saved his money and married Alberta Huber in 1933.

Alberta Huber and John Roach engaged in 1932 and married in 1933

Their honeymoon made the front page of the Union City newspapers as money was so tight during the depression, that is was unusual for young people to cruise to Bermuda as they did on the Cunard ship *Monarch of the Seas*.

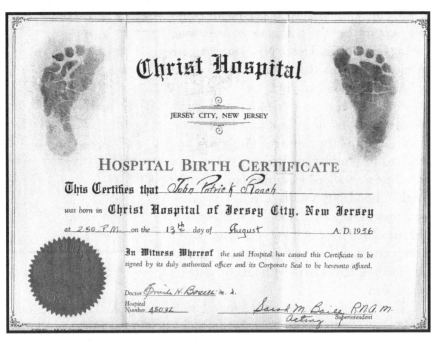

Little did I know that these feet are made for exploring the world.

Baby John, 1936

I was born in 1936.

My first memories are of playing in a sand pile next to the new home my parents were having built in Fail Lawn, NJ . They had me memorize 603 Fairlawn Parkway, to tell a policeman in case I got lost.

By 1941 my best friends were Egon Mueller and his little brother Herbie who lived around the corner. America was involved in World War II during these years and there was talk of a German family in the neighborhood, but nothing came of it as they were truly American. Barbara Walters was my girl friend and lived only two doors away. My world consisted of going around the block and not crossing any streets without my parents permission.

Grandpa says, "Take one step at a time"

The spirit of adventure started for me at about age four. First I discussed the idea of running away from home with my parents; they agreed and said it was a good idea. Mom made me a peanut butter and jelly sandwich and a thermos bottle of milk. They escorted me to the front door and kissed me good by at about 4:00 pm in the afternoon. They asked if I wanted a sweater on this nice summer evening and being so independent I refused.

I really felt good about being on my own, I walked around the block and visited Egon and Herbie, I told them I just ran away from home. They were really impressed. We played outside for awhile until they got called in for dinner, so I went to call on Barbara only two houses from home. Barbara could not come out so I sat on the curb in front of her house and ate my peanut butter and jelly sandwich.

Eventually is started to get dark, and finally the street lights went on. It was a beautiful evening with a half moon and lots of stars. I felt secure sitting on the curb under the street light but I was

Dad and I at the beach in Leonardo, NJ

4

starting to get tired. I got up and walked to Barbara's house and rang the doorbell, when Mrs. Walters answered, I told her I ran away from home and needed a place to sleep. She told me my mother was visiting her and to come in and have some cookies.

The next morning I woke up in my own bed having my first adventure behind me as a proven fiasco by a little independent kid.

Johnny, Barbara Walters, Herbie and Egon Muller

chapter ii
KINDERGARTEN

As I approach five years old, my dad went to the town fathers and appealed to them to have the school bus that takes the children to the public school, continue to the private Catholic school as well, and the town fathers agreed.

My first day of school was a memorable one. A whole bunch of us kids waiting on the corner with their mothers for the school bus. Some of us were given instructions not to get off at the first stop because that was the public school, but to stay on the bus for the Catholic School.

First day of school, here's johnny, standing on the curb waiting for bus.

Upon arrival I was assigned to the kindergarten class and a child that was afraid to have his mother leave him with nuns put on a demonstration of screaming. The nuns told the mother to bring the kid back next year. My first experience with nuns was don't mess with nuns or they could send you home for a year, besides they were dressed in black, wore funny clothes and were boss.

About six of us were first to use this newly scheduled bus that on that on the return trip after school would stop at the public school to pick up the majority of pupils. I was obvious to me that the public school kids had more fun than the kids at my school.

By the end of the first week, I made another one of my infamous decisions, to get off the bus at the public school. I asked my friend Egon what to do, as he would show me to the Kindergarten with his little brother Herbie. I entered and took a seat, the quite beautiful young teacher asked who I was and what am I doing here.

*Hey! Now I have a sister,
Carol Ann Roach*

"My name is John P. Roach Jr.,, I live at 603 Fairlawn parkway and I would like to change Kindergartens as I don't like my Kindergarten."

This lovely teacher called the principal who called the Catholic School and before you knew it a station wagon full of angry nuns came to pick me up at the public school. Deep do, do's, I'm in I guess, as they showed their anger and they told me my father will be angry when I get home.

After all, it was my father that organized this bus for the Catholic kids in the neighborhood. I got home and my mother says "Wait until your father gets home."

Which is worse, angry nuns or an angry father? Angry nuns for sure, they smack you with rulers across your knuckles. My father has such a big heart, he fakes being mad to teach me a lesson, but down deep he hides his smile knowing his son is already a free thinker.

I was the smallest of all the kids in Kindergarten, and was chosen to lead the May Procession at the parish church to crown the Virgin Mary attended by hundreds of people. So on rare occasion I made my parents proud.

I had two girlfriends at this school, Mary Lou and Alice, I liked them both and vied for their attention. Alice actually took me home for lunch to meet her mother. I had no idea what to do with these beauties. Maybe kiss em, that's about it. Mom organized a surprise birthday party for me and invited the parents of Mary Lou and Alice to bring their kids.

Egon and Herbie and Barbara Walters were there and my baby sister Carol three years younger than I, and Mary Lou and Alice so the party must have looked like your typical an *Our Gang Movie*.

John and Carol at 603 Fairlawn Parkway.

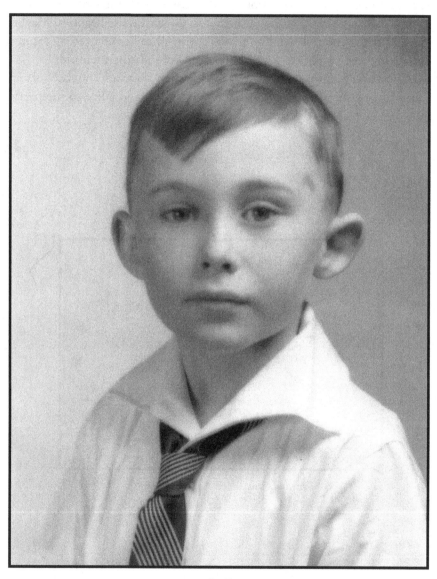

Age 7

chapter iii
GLEN ROCK, NJ

IN THE summer before the second grade, my parents bought a larger older home in Glen Rock, NJ; a beautiful town,where most people worked in Manhattan, New York City and commuted each day by train.

I entered my first public school. Yes, public! Richard E. Byrd School named for the great explorer of Antarctica. My first teacher was the beautiful Mrs. White in the second grade. I was not a good student and rebelled against any form of regimentation, but somehow survived. The only subjects that I was interested in were geography, history and reading books of my own choice.

Our new home, 15 Kent Road, Glen Rock, NJ

I read my first book given to me by my father's sister, Aunt Marian. The title *The Boxcar Children* by Gertrude Chandler Warner was intriguing and I was fascinated by these young children on their own and independent living in a boxcar. I think my Aunt Marian could see right through me and always seemed to know my wants and needs before I knew them myself.

My Grandfather whom I loved very much slipped and fell on a freshly

John, Carol and James Roach, Ages 8, 5 and baby.

varnished floor and broke his hip and died the same day. I saw my father cry and I cried. Within a day or two I realized that I too shall eventually die. In fact, I concluded, you are born and you die --- and it is what you accomplish between these two dates, that is what life is all about.

I'm pretty young to have thoughts like this, so what can I accomplish? Adventure! Yes, I'm still a kid and don't know much, but for sure adventure is something I can start right now after all, ---------Life Is For Living.

My closest friend was Bobby Hohorst who lived around the block. We would explore things together. Both of us were the same age and size at age 7, in fact we were diminutive, tiny kids for our age, we looked more like age 5 and people thought we were cute little boys.

There was an undeveloped hill a block away with only weeds growing on it. When we climbed it and looked to the east we could see the New York City Skyline, the Empire State Building and the George Washington Bridge only eight miles away.

Looking to the west was a shallow mountain range of inspiring cliffs that captured our imagination beyond the next town of Hawthorne, NJ and probably further yet in North Haledon are cliffs that we could hike to for both adventure and to express our independence. The adolescent life can be pretty boring unless you seek adventure. So we did and it was always fun, we approached the cliffs in a different way each time we hiked.

Below the cliffs were private residences, we would have to cross someone's property to get to the cliffs. As we walked parallel to the cliffs, a hairy giant dog came out to meets us. A big white hairy dog, probably weighed more than us little kids, with so much hair covering his eyes we wondered how he could see. This large dog was barking so much that the owner came out and saw two terrified little boys not daring to move.

"That's Robert, my dog, he won't hurt you, he is an English Sheep Dog" the man said. We asked if we could cross his property to get to the mountains. He said, "anytime you want, Robert will come out to greet you, each time, so don't be afraid."

Robert and us little kids became good friends. Each time we went to the mountains Robert came out to greet us. We always pet him and roughed him up, sometimes giving him a dog biscuit. I guess Robert looked forward to our visits, because he always seemed so happy to see us.

My idealism started to surface at this young age. I became a free thinker. If you don't like something, change it to something you do like. Adventure was my way of coping with the regimentation of going to school every day. I prefer to learn only what I am interested in, rather than from organized curriculums for the masses.

During these years my hobby was collecting stamps from around the world, just like President FDR and with my globe I was able to find and name every country and its capital. I noticed that the circumnavigation route of Magellan was clearly marked on the globe and dreamed that someday I will experience the same adventure. My favorite TV program was Lowell Thomas with his travels to obscure countries, like Tibet, Siam and the Asian and African Countries.

Adventure became a very important part of my childhood, between collecting stamps and learning about foreign countries and Lowell Thomas on TV I became interested in seeing the world for myself. A family showed slides to the students at school that they took visiting many National Parks and I decided right then, that some day I will visit the National Parks.

There were only two deterrents to my simple adventure life style, school which I abhorred and mowing the lawn. Our Glen Rock home was on ½ acre of green well manicured grass. My parents wanted a nice looking yard so I was elected full time lawn mower. They did not have sit down mowers in those days, the best we had was a rope start 18 inch noisy power mower.

By the time the front and side yard was finished the backyard needed mowing and vice versa. I was always mowing and it occurred to me, why have grass? You cut it, it grows again. Cut it again, it grows again and again and again. What a waste of a human life! I do this because it is my responsibility to my parents, but when I grow up, I will not tolerate a single blade of grass.

Okay, I ask myself, what is the ideal? Simple, a wooded lot, pure nature, no grass. Ha! Now all I have to do is grow up. I passed these views on to my parents who thought I thought I should be more pragmatic rather than idealistic, as there are no wooded lots in Glen Rock.

Banished to a life of cutting grass, is like fighting nature. I accepted my lot in purgatory but really couldn't smile knowing the grass would still be growing there long after I am dead.

As a Cub Scout I learned all about camping out and earned my wolf, bear and lion badges with gold and two silver arrows for each that kept my mom busy sewing. Got my Webelos and continued on to the Boy Scouts where even today I can still recite the oath.

I do have a way of bringing out the worst in people, probably because even at a very young age I was so sure of myself, it causes in some the urge, to want to put me down.

Boy Scout

Miss Innes, my fifth grade teacher requested many parent teacher meetings with my parents convincing my parents that I am some sort of a dummy. My parents were torn between believing the teacher or their son. My father's sister Marian Roach who eventually retired as Superintendent of Schools for Union City, NJ graduated from Columbia University with an Education major and had all her course work done for PhD offered to have me tested, so my father consented.

My final grade in the fifth grade with Miss Innes was an F (Failure) in every subject, who recommended that I be left back. My Aunt Marian Roach stepped in to tell my parents not to let them leave me back, because he probably is just bored with his teachers as he tested genius on his IQ.

Freckle Face Age 12

chapter iv

MOBILITY

By the time I was ten or eleven had a paper route for the Bergen Evening Record and using my bike delivered newspapers to about 40 customers, The bicycle also expanded my range of exploration and adventure. By the time I was 13, my sister Carol and I rode from Glen Rock, NJ, 8 miles to the George Washington Bridge, crossed the bridge, leaving our initials on the dividing line sign between New Jersey and New York in the middle of the bridge and continued to the New York side.

At age 13 Mom took me for my first airplane ride over Glen Rock and New York City.

Having crossed the bridge brother and sister, found Broadway and traveled from 181st[th] street south through Harlem all the way to Times Square where we ate Macaroni & Cheese in Horn & Hardart Automat Restaurant for .25 cents, before we turned around and headed home.

What an adventure, New York City with my little sister, as we tried to get home by 5:00 pm. My dad wasn't expected home until 6:15 and we both arrived at 6:00 with dinner ready just waiting for Dad.

"Where have you been, you are both late?." Mom asked.

"Just riding around on our bikes", said Carol.

chapter v

INTRODUCTION TO CLASSICAL MUSIC

By THE seventh grade I entered Glen Rock Junior High School where the course work was very exciting. Mrs. Waterhouse, my favorite teacher instilled in me a love for classical music and opera. She started with Prokovfiev's *Peter and the Wolf* where we learned the sound of each instrument and moved on to The Sorcerers Apprentice, Grand Canyon Suite, Beethoven's 5th, each of which utilized the entire orchestra.

She also had the entire class singing arias from various operas. I just couldn't wait to attend her next class. So fortunate was I for two years to have a teacher like Mrs. Waterhouse.

My father took a second job at Columbia Record Club more for the purpose of accruing quarters needed for Social Security for his future retirement in addition to his government retirement program.

I sure benefited from his tenure at Columbia Record Club because he brought home so many 78rpm LP (long playing) Classical Music Albums. With Mrs. Waterhouse instilling in me at school the enjoyment of the masters and with Dads albums, I was able to reinforce my learning curve exponentially. At first I had no trained ear but could really appreciate Haydn's Trumpet Concerto. I realized that the recording that I have is with trumpets with no valves that added to the mystique.

My art teacher had me copying The Mill at Wyk in watercolors that I gave my mom as a gift.

The shop teacher had me cut out on a band saw a 15 inch pig on 1 inch thick popular for a bread board. Mom loved it. He also had me turn a lamp on the lathe that I coated with oil giving it a rich teak color and on a drill press cut a hole for the wire to light a bulb at the top. I purchased a lamp shade and electric plug to finish it off.

chapter vi

HIGH SCHOOL

THE CLICHÉ, all good things must come to an end happened to me as my parents enrolled me in St. Luke's High School, a Catholic school in Ho-Ho-Kus, NJ.

The first day of High School, in the Phys Ed class, they asked everyone in the ninth grade to line up by height. To my disgrace I was shorter than the shortest girl.

What a way to start a new school, I was enrolled in college prep, which means I had to take 2 years of Latin, 2 years of French, 4 years of Religion, Math, Science and a year of Chemistry, none of which, did I have an interest. Talk about boring? My classmates would recite, "Latin is a language is dead as can be, first it killed the Romans and now it is killing me." I pretty much had to memorize *Caesar's Gallic Wars* to pass Latin.

As a student I was a disaster, totally not interested in the regimentation of high school. Outside of school I was quite industrious. I took a job and supported myself as a part time grocery clerk at .50 cents an hour after school and weekends at the A & P super market. I knew the price of everything in the store so they made me a check out person at the register. I even joined the *Amalgamated Meat Cutters and Butchers Workman's Union*, that got me a 50% raise to .75 cents per hour.

Before you knew it I was making $1.00 per hour and had a goal of buying my first car when I became 17 years old. I completely supported myself since my first day of high school by never asking my parents for anything, in fact my Dad required that I pay room and board to teach me the discipline of responsibility.

Mom and Dad also purchased a baby grand piano for the living room and wanted me to take piano lessons. Of course I rebelled, as with high school and work at the A&P after school I had no time for more regimentation.

As it was I had to take two busses to High School, Bus #72 to Ridgewood, NJ that change busses to Ho-Ho-Kus to St. Luke's High School. I would leave home early without breakfast get bus 72 and meet friends for breakfast at Ligget's Drug Store in Ridgewood. Breakfast was routine, lots of coffee with an English Muffin, with Joyce Clark, Vinney McCarthy, Tom Roemer, Joe Ciappera, Marge McTighe and Cecilia Corcoran.

I went on a date with Cel Corcoran and she walked me to the bus stop in Ridgewood on my way home. She held my hand as I got on the bus and with the door still open pulled me off the bus to give me my first real kiss. The bus driver waited, laughing at my surprise.

Two days later in the Ridgewood bus terminal, I found Cel in a cat fight over me with another gal saying, "he is mine" while rolling around on the floor and punching out the other gal. Good for my ego, I guess, let them fight over me.

Joyce Clark, in high school took the time to teach me how to dance. I guess I was pretty square to gain the attention of these two women at my age 16 that for both it turns out to have lasted a lifetime.

In both cases above it might have been my first experience with women, except maybe for Laura Larkin.

Laura Larkin was my Confirmation partner in Mt. Carmel Church in Ridgewood, NJ. When I first saw her before we walked down the aisle together she looked like my future bride with her blonde hair flowing, her pale white skin, beautiful smile and fluttering eyes, wearing in what looked like a wedding dress. I was smitten.

I probably was still quite the nerd, more interested in cars than girls, and still had a lot of growing up to do.

chapter vii

WHEELS

My FATHER's sister Marian Roach always kept an eye on me and as I approached age 17 she asked my father if it would be all right if she gave me her immaculate 1938 Pontiac. This car was simonized at least once a week by my grandfather and had only 20,000 miles on it. I wish I still had this car today. My father insisted that this car not be given to me, and that it would be good discipline that I pay for my first car. My aunt said okay and settled on a price of $50.00.

Now with my own car I could pick up Laura on my way to school, that I planned to do every day. To my surprise Laura comes from a very wealthy family and lives in quite the mansion in Ridgewood, NJ.

1938 Pontiac with my classmates, photo from 1954 School Yearbook.

Any time off from school or work was spent enjoying my Pontiac. My parents enjoyed my friends visiting with their cars in our driveway with the hoods of the cars up while we compared engines. I actually removed the side panels of the engine compartment and painted the engine silver with a red Pontiac Indian on the side with chrome bolt covers and accessories.

The car attracted so many police that one officer who pulled me over said, "we know what time you leave every morning and your exact route to pick up your girl friend so wise up, slow down, put the side panels back on and become a good citizen."

I guess I was too shy and too much involved in my car and work and just content and grateful to have Laura as a best female pal.

Occasionally Laura would have classmates over to her home to play pool in their wood paneled den. Her mom would answer the door and always welcomed each of us. One day I took Laura out to lunch during school and stopped too abruptly in front of a mall restaurant where people were walking.

In class that afternoon I saw a police car pull up to the front door of the school and shortly thereafter heard the announcement, "John Roach, please report to the principal's office."

Upon arriving at the principal's office I was presented with a summons to court by a citizens arrest for a traffic violation and removal of my driver's license for careless driving. I was young enough to actually think I could successfully defend myself against the cranky citizen filing the summons.

To make a long story short, the evening arrived that I was to appear in court and to my surprise, Laura was there with her mother to see my embarrassment of publicly losing my license for 30 days over a citizen's complaint. Cést la vie. Accept it and move on with a lesson learned, I thought, but how nice and considerate it was, that mother and daughter were there to help if needed.

Months later, as my life resumed Laura said, "My father wants to meet you, so come over tomorrow night." Mother answered the door with Laura at her side and introduced me to Mr. Larkin who was very cordial. He said, Laura is about to enter society and I would like you to accompany her to the Cotillion at Ridgewood Country Club.

He offered to pay for everything including tuxedo rental and a limousine. I let him know that I already have a tux and my 1938 Pontiac is ample transportation. He asked, why would I have a tux at such a young age? I told him that I have a part time job a Donahue's, a fancy restaurant on Route 23, that requires it's waiters to own a tuxedo. He laughed and saw where I was coming from, an independent kid, totally unaware of my lower social status; he shook my hand and said okay.

Laura

Laura was her beautiful perfect self as the valet opened the doors of my 1938 Pontiac to allow us to enter the Country Club, followed immediately by her parents in the limousine.

This Cotillion was an eye opening experience for me. Most of the male guests were the famous sons of somebody, like sons of chairman's of the board of various companies, or sons of fathers with seats on the stock exchange. I was just me! I had little in common with the males around me, only my love for Laura. I stood by while others asked her to dance and when she was available I danced with her.

It was an interesting evening and a complete learning experience for me. Laura had a good time and entered high society like the princess she was and never lost her sense of humor. As we left the Cotillion I mentioned how easy it would be for the valet to find my car amongst the Jaguars, Cadillac's and Rolls Royce's.

I continued to pick up Laura every day for school, my sister Carol often came with us and the two of them got along fine. Laura was one year ahead of me and was already planning to go to Loretta Heights College, in Colorado Springs, Colorado, so I had to prepare myself for my Senior Year without Laura.

chapter viii

MILITARY SERVICE

WHILE STILL a junior in High School I became interested in the New Jersey National Guard, with all their jeeps, tanks, army trucks and a promise of travel to the thousand islands on the St. Lawrence River and visits to Kingston, Ontario, that would be my first trip to another country, Canada.

Having never really traveled any distance, the promise of two weeks training at Camp Drum, near Watertown, NY each year sounded exciting, so I signed up knowing that such action would complete my military service obligation and provide some travel and adventure at the same time.

The National Guard provided me with both fatigue and dress uniforms as well as Army Truck driver training for the 250 mile drive to Camp Drum for each summer encampment. I learned all the Army stuff, like never ask the sergeant to go to the PX because the answer is no. Just go to the PX and if questioned, take the consequences.

Most sentences by the sergeant start with, "All right you guys", field strip the area, i.e. pick up everything that doesn't grow.

As our convoy approached Camp Drum after two nights bivouac in designated empty fields. We see the barracks that we will have to clean with a tooth brush or similar device., for our inspection each day.

When off duty I visited Kingston, Ontario Canada, so my limited world at age 17 has now expanded to include my first visit to another country.

I was in the 50 Armored Division, Corps of Engineers in Charlie

Company, who's job during the two weeks training was to build a wooden bridge to cross a ravine capable of supporting tanks to cross. We completed the bridge, tanks crossed it successfully and then blew up the bridge. Demolition I learned is also a responsibility of the Corps of Engineers and part of this training exercise.

I learned very much on this trip. They made coffee in a giant pot of boiling water with coffee in the bottom with no separation between and scooped the coffee of the top. Cream and sugar were not available, so for the first time in my life I learned how to drink black coffee, and have done so ever since.

PFC Roach

Hundreds of people can be fed fast with garbage cans full of boiling water containing K-rations (typical canned food like Ravioli) for meals in the field. Actually, I did like the variety.

chapter ix

SENIOR YEAR AT ST.LUKE'S HIGH SCHOOL

WITH LAURA off to college and me still plodding through high school I was pretty lonesome until I met Joyce Borell. Thank goodness for Joyce whom I nick-named Bo Bo and who was pretty much on my mind throughout my senior year.

Joyce would take me home to teach me more dance technique that she saw on Dick Clark TV Shows. Her mother watched and often clapped and encouraged us to continue. Joyce and I had no trouble winning dance contests at St. Luke's High School.

Her parents were against her riding in my car and my parents were afraid we would get too serious. Both parents finally relented and Bo Bo became my primary date through my Senior Year, with nothing serious because I was still very immature.

During my senior year the nuns chose me to be the master of ceremonies for most events with the whole school in attendance in the auditorium. With this experience I was exposed to fearless public speaking at an early age and attained a confidence that would last me a lifetime.

My room, Dad and Mom refinishing my desk, Dad hung that exquisite wallpaper.

At the end of my senior year, I wasn't sure I would graduate as I got a 3 on my chemistry exam because there was only 97 questions. So getting a three was a gift. To my surprise they called out John P Roach Jr., for his diploma, my final report card had a few erasures on it, so I guess they figured I suffered enough. I chuckled when they started giving out scholarly medals to students for Math, English, Science, etc., because I knew I was eligible for nothing.

My wallet photo of my parents.

When they finally got done with the academic awards they called out John P. Roach Jr. for the *School Spirit Award*. My parents were so proud of their son. My Dad said of all the awards given you got a prestigious award that will get you into college. He told me he would lend me the money for college if I chose a Catholic College.

The following summer was spent looking at colleges and I chose St. Michael's College, in Colchester near Burlington, Vermont. I was very excited and why not? A dumb kid like me going to College.

chapter x

COLLEGE YEARS

IN 1956 St. Michaels College was a College for men only. Gals came in for dances and other activities from Trinity College or University of Vermont in nearby Burlington.

I was a waiter in Burlington, Vermont restaurants to help pay for my education. I was on the SMC Ski Team, Track Team and Cross Country Team. I would run 10 miles a day to stay in shape for cross country which is why they wanted me on the ski team. My first attempt at cross-country skiing was a disaster in a multi collegiate event at Paul Smiths College in Saranac Lake NY.

Everyone got a number and started 15 seconds apart. As the most novice I wore number 1 and started first, number 2 passed me about 20 seconds later, then numbers 3 and 4. Before you knew it, numbers 20 and 21 passed me and I was getting tired. All my team mates eventually passed me so I got nervous and fell a few times trying to catch up. Eventually number 52 passed me and there was no one left and it was snowing and the tracks of everyone before me were already covered.

It was getting dark as I got within sight of the finish line I could see that everyone had already gone home except my team mates waiting by their station wagon. Another team mate who did the course twice looking for number 1 was coming up behind me watching me fend off barking dogs with my ski poles as I crossed the finish line exhausted.

In my Junior year I broke my leg skiing and met Jacqueline Frenette in a Winooski Diner while on crutches. I asked her out to the dance on Saturday Night, She looked at my crutches, smiled and said yes! The two of us hit it off with the same sense of humor and we became an item on campus for the remainder of my junior year attending every campus function together.

Jackie, one of ten children in the Frenette family took me home to meet her parents. Both her parents took me in as if I was their eleventh. This was my first experience with a family so large, I was continually invited to dinner and they often said there is always room for one more. Stella and Pop Frenette were like my Vermont mother and father.

The Frenette family were descendents of French Canadians who came to Vermont to work in the woolen mills. Jackie did not speak English until she was six years old as both her household and her school were French speaking.

-Junior Weekend, with Jackie, St. Michael's College.
Les Elgart Orchestra, famous for Night Train.

Having already completed a Philosophy Major at Seton Hall University, I returned to St. Michael's College in my Junior Year and majored in Political Science requiring me to take both the Sophomore and Junior Political Sciences classes.

I found bad Karma with my Sophomore Political Science Teacher who appeared to be very satisfied with my studies as I was carrying an A throughout the year in his department. I let him know that I had to miss a class to attend the NCAA Basketball, Small College Championship where SMC was in contention and if need be, I would do extra work to make up for the class missed. Dr. Spencer advised me not to go to SMC in the final four of the NCAA Finals.

Lake Champlain Beach Party with Jackie.

Six students including myself crammed in a car painted with Evansville, Indiana or bust to cheer our team to victory where we came in third in the nation behind Evansville and North Dakota. By doing so I chose adventure over unscrupulous discipline for blind obedience rather than continued proficiency in political science not realizing the penalty Dr. Spencer had in mind.

The result of this action was an F in sophomore Political Science compared to an A in junior level political science both taken the same year. I tried to reason with the professor Dr. Spencer to no avail as an F in my major is a cause for flunking out of school.

Did I learn from this experience? I sure did! A Political Science lesson on how to deal with a totalitarian autocratic dictator showing his violent power to punish rather than his ability to educate. Although he was also a Vermont State Senator at the time, I accepted my grade of F and came to see what a little man he really was.

Highest ROTC Rank in Class, that's me in front of College Band, most forward, Parents proud.

ST. Michael's College, Oklahoma Weekend.

chapter xi

MANAGEMENT TRAINING

WITH SUMMER coming I rented an apartment in Burlington to be near my girlfriend Jackie Frenette and was hired by Franchi Construction Company of West Newton MA to be their Burlington, VT office Manager. Mr. Ibey, their Superintendent took a liking to me and had me trained in their Massachusetts HQ, to be the office manager.

Each day at work Jackie's mother, Stella Frenette would send one of her daughters to Franchi Construction Co, with lunch that she made for me. I guess I became the 11th kid and loved every minute of it. Three other students were my roommates in a nifty apartment on the top floor at the foot of Church Street. From our 6th floor window we could see all the activity on Burlington's main drag all the way to the Church at the top of Church Street.

Near the end of this wonderful summer, my father showed up, surveying my situation with three male roommates and me with a good job, living near my girlfriend, to whom I have already fallen in love.

My dad tried to convince me to return home to Glen Rock, NJ. The logic he used, included the income would be greater in New Jersey, you can continue school at Farleigh Dickenson, University, visit your girlfriend in Vermont on weekends and get on with your life without the need of room mates. Furthermore, an opportunity to pay back my Dad for the college loan he gave me so he can start saving for my younger sister's college education.

My Dad went home without me but I gave his suggestions a lot of thought. I certainly felt an obligation to Mr. Ibey who set me up with the most perfect job and gave me so much confidence and training that I felt obligated to stay.

Mr. Ibey, my first mentor, whom I trusted completely, assured me that he could train another student to take my place and my father was giving me good sound advice for the future. His job would be in Burlington only while the project lasted building the Federal Building and when completed, move to another city in New England when another project was contracted. He said I should use him as a reference anytime.

My next obligation was the Frenette family. I asked Pop Frenette for permission to marry his daughter. He laughed and said, "took you long enough, only nine more to go."

It was nearing September 1958 and we planned a wedding for Thanksgiving Day 1959, so it was a sad day when I departed Vermont for New Jersey with plans to visit Jackie on weekends whenever possible.

chapter xii
ALASKA

THE FIRST job in New Jersey that I applied for I got. My experience as Office manager with Mr. Ibey certainly helped me land a job with my new manager Herman Moritz of ITT Federal Electric Corporation who hired me as Manager of the DEWLine Technical Library with a salary of $80.00 per week, considered a good salary at that time.

It didn't take me long to make the most of this job. There was a series of 71 radar installations across the Arctic from Alaska to Greenland, to provide a Distant Early Warning of any possible attack from the north on the United States. May job was to insure that each of the 71 installations had up to date manuals.

With a staff of five I set up 71 branch libraries at each radar station from a headquarters n Paramus, NJ. By year end 1959 my salary was increased to $100.00 per week. That was a lot of money at that time. I bought a low mileage powder blue 1952 Cadillac Convertible with a white top and dark blue leather seats. I would impress my friends with the gas tank under the rear tail light that popped up to fill the tank.

I would visit Jackie religiously at least every two weeks from Friday night through Monday morning when I would arrive back very tired as the trip is 700 miles round trip. During the week I was taking a course in Psychology from Dr. Murray Banks at Farleigh Dickenson University in Teaneck, NJ in addition to my National Guard duty every Tuesday night, so I was quite maxed out. On Christmas Day I gave Jackie her 1 carat blue white diamond engagement ring set between two diamond baggets.

General Saleen, a retired military officer was on the staff of ITT Federal Electric Corporation who often complemented me on the job I was doing. In his office he had various certificates stating that he crossed the Arctic Circle and visited the DEWLine that I admired.

One day the General said:

"How would you like to visit the DEWLine?"

"Adventure! Me! Yes, General, I can't wait."

I have another mentor General Saleen, who made all the arrangements. My parents were elated, but my mother questioned my leaving for Alaska in March with just a raincoat, but I assured her the Air Force would provide me with sub-zero Arctic gear.

I was booked first class on Northwest Airlines from New York to Seattle a propeller aircraft that took 8 hours in those days. Stayed at the Olympic Hotel in Seattle for a morning flight to Anchorage on Wein Alaska Airlines.

Upon my arrival in Anchorage, Alaska with a population of only 40,000 at that time I was amazed to arrive on statehood week in March of 1959. Remnants of the bonfire celebration were still to be found. The first evening at the hotel, I experienced my first earthquake, the chandeliers were swinging, but Alaskans are used to them. I was really impressed with the silk sheets at the hotel.

Three days later after my Anchorage experience it was Wein Alaska Airlines again for a flight to Fairbanks where I was to stay at a BOQ, Bachelor's Officers Quarters at Ladd Air force Base where I was given the designated rank of Major and issued Arctic Gear. General Saleen sure is taking good care of me, I thought.

Fairbanks in 1959 was like a wild West Town, only the main street was paved, all the cross streets were dirt, although covered with hard pack snow. I was able to pet a baby polar bear, and visited the University of Alaska to see a 9 foot stuffed grizzly bear that was quite intimidating. I also spent a day skiing at the Fairbanks ski bowl. Fairbanks allowed me to experience the American Frontier.

A few days in Fairbanks and now on a private plane bound for Point Barrow Alaska. The plane was airborne only 15 minutes when the pilot announced we have too much ice on the wings and are making an emergency landing by returning to Fairbanks for de-icing.

The second attempt was more successful, flying over the Brooks Range was an awesome experience. Landing at Point Barrow on the shores of the Arctic Ocean was interesting, as I could see the Eskimo Village right before me.

I was picked up at Barrow Airport by a yellow heated half track vehicle with skis in the front and delivered to the Point Barrow Main DEWLine radar site. A warm welcome was arranged for me by General Saleen, who obviously tracked my every destination.

My Arctic Gear allowed visits in 52 degrees below zero in March.

Most of the ITT employees at these sites have at least an 18 month contract at very high pay because they are away from their families. To keep morale up, they have excellent chef's preparing wonderful dishes and various entertainment. This DEWLine site is within walking distance to the Point Barrow Eskimo Village. Typical March weather is 52 degrees below zero. If it warms up a little I would like to visit the village.

Days later, dressed in my arctic gear I left the DEWLine site and walked to the Eskimo Village at Point Barrow. As I approached the village, what looked like two wolves approached me and I stood very still quite frightened, until an Eskimo said, "relax they are my husky's used for my dog sled." I noticed caribou stored on the roof of some of the wooden homes and realized, why not, an outdoor freezer.

I passed the hotel called "The Top of the World Hotel" and looked inside to find it warm and comfortable. Further down the main street of the village was a modern building used by scientists for arctic research where they were feeding a baby polar bear.

Top Of The World Hotel, Point Barrow, Alaska

At the very point of Point Barrow on the frozen Arctic Ocean, I saw the monument commemorating the last flight of Will Rogers and Wiley Post, lost in the Arctic. This impressive monument made me aware that exploring the world can be very exciting, but can also be dangerous.

Returning to the comfort of the Point Barrow DEWLine Main Site that is 500 miles from the next Main Site with many smaller DEWLine sites in between. My responsibility was to make sure all 71 Branch Libraries at each radar site had up to date technical manuals. I accomplished this by delegating responsibility to the Main sites for delivery of manuals to the smaller sites in between.

My itinerary dictated that I visit another main site 500 miles to the east at Barter Island, Alaska for a few days to have the experience of at least two main sites.

As the aircraft approached the landing strip at Barter Island, I was amazed at the view before me. The landing strip was marked with lots of wrecked aircraft on both sides, on the beach of the Arctic Ocean. Actually not a bad idea as everything is white, and the landing strip is clearly marked with various bright colors of wrecked aircraft. I wondered what the pilot thinks while landing between all these crashed aircraft.

Barter Island also had a nearby Eskimo Village, although not as large as at Point Barrow. The DEWLIne site was identical to the previous one and those working there every bit as hospitable. Eventually it became time to leave the DEWLine and return to Fairbanks. I was given the option to return from Alaska any way that suited me.

At Fairbanks Airport I saw the Pan American Clipper, a two level aircraft with the wing on top. I inquired and was told they referred to it as the milk run to Seattle because it stopped at so many places and takes longer.

In the spirit of Adventure, I booked passage of the Pan Am Clipper, flying to White Horse, the Capital of the Yukon, Canada where I spent some time on the ground then taking off again to Juneau, Alaska's Capital and Ketchikan, a fishing village surrounded by mountains on its way to Seattle. I thoroughly enjoyed the ambience of this clipper ship sitting upstairs with cocktails and hors d'Oeuvres before dinner.

My return to New York City from Seattle was my first of many future flights on the TWA Constellation, an aircraft that will remain classic with me forever. The days of aircraft dinners served on fine china, with monogrammed silverware and passengers that would not even consider traveling without dressing for the occasion are long gone. I was so fortunate to take part in this era of tasteful travel.

Returning to ITT Federal Electric Corporation and my mentor General Saleen in Paramus, NJ, I was so thankful to the General for this wondrous experience that he is often mentioned in my books as a profound mentor in my life. He has expanded my exploration horizons from the 1000 Islands of New York State to Point Barrow, Alaska in the very year of Alaska Statehood.

chapter xiii

PLANNING A FUTURE

Now BACK to reality, I visit Jackie whom I love and will eventually be my wife to let her know the excitement of such a wonderful idealistic travel experience. We make plans for when we are married to try to go on a travel adventure vacation together at least once a year. I drive the round trip of 700 miles to visit Jackie just about every two weeks as we plan our wedding for Thanksgiving Day.

Another interest that I developed was sports car racing with my pals Al and Brian. We travel to various venues during these years whenever possible. One of the nicest sports car race courses I have ever been to is in Lime Rock Connecticut. Standing on a hill in the center of the course, you can see the entire race.

My mom was so surprised when I asked my little brother Jimmy if he wanted to come to the Lime Rock Sports Car Race. Jimmy is eight years younger and had a day that he always remembered with his big brother.

I had so many interests in life that it was easy for me at age 23 to remain a virgin until my wedding day.

Jackie and I were married in St. Francis Church, the French Church in Winooski, Vermont with a reception at nearby Sunny Hollow and left for our Honeymoon to Chateau Frontenac in Quebec City, Canada. With dinner at the famous Beaver Club in Montreal we stayed overnight at the Queen Elizabeth Hotel, in Montreal before heading for Quebec City the next day.

From Montreal to Quebec City is a pretty drive along the St. Lawrence

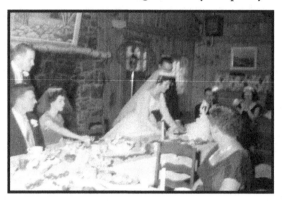

Jackie cuts the wedding cake.

River as you pass each town you can't help but notice the largest building is always the church and eventually you can see the Chateau Frontenac and impressive castle like structure built by the Canadian Pacific Railroad as one of the many European Style Hotels they built in many Provinces across Canada.

Being young at heart the newlyweds could laugh at the simplest of things. At dinner at the Chateau for example, a drop of spinach no bigger than a BB was noticed by our waiter who returned with a blade, that I thought he would lift up this tiny green BB off the table. He chose to spread the greenness of the spinach BB all over the place trying to clean it up. After apologizing profusely he changed the table cloth in the middle of our dinner.

The accompanying violins only added to this show as the violinists joined Jackie and I in laughter at this pathetic sight of over-zealous attention to the spinach.

Quebec City is very European, perhaps the only walled city in North America. The primary language is French, so Jackie being bilingual was very comfortable here. We walked on top of the walls, visited the lower city on the funicular, strolled the promenade all

Chateau Frontenac

the way to the Citadel and got involved in the history of the French Canadians and the plains of Abraham that eventually caused the defeat of the French by the British.

The restaurants of Quebec City are another marvel, Les Ancien Canadian tops the list for Canadian food while French Cuisine is everywhere. My French speaking improved a lot with Jackie's help, I certainly could read every menu and had my first l'éscargot.

Leaving the Chateau Frontenac we returned to our new apartment in Hawthorne, NJ, by traveling south to Skowhegan Maine then west through New Hampshire to Lake Champlain Vermont and south to Hawthorne, NJ. So we both were very much in love and did a lot of sight seeing on our Honeymoon.

Having such a good time on our honeymoon we both decided, that if financially possible we would plan a trip each year that would add to the adventure in life.

When summer came during our first year living in New Jersey we did what Jersey people do, make many trips to the Jersey Shore. We often spent weekends on the beach at Seaside Heights or Point Pleasant.

chapter xiv
NOVA SCOTIA &
MARATIME PROVINCES

By MID-SUMMER it was time to take an extended vacation and in our first year of marriage, we decided on Cavendish Beach, Prince Edward Island, Canada. This choice was quite an adventure. We drove to Acadia National Park in Maine and were quite impressed as it was the first National Park for both of us. The ocean was icy cold but the park was beautiful.

We stayed overnight in Bar Harbor Maine and were scheduled to take the Bluenose Car Ferry across the Bay of Fundy to Nova Scotia the next morning. Little did I know I would be so seasick, Jackie held up better than I.

We drove along the Atlantic Coast through many fishing villages until we came to London, Nova Scotia where we stayed overnight at a B&B. We visited a town square with an unusual monument of a battle where the US lost to the British. So our eyes are now opened for new experiences.

The next day we entered and toured Halifax, especially noteworthy was the fort overlooking the big harbor. We found a B&B and made reservations for the evening and went to a Pub. Upon entering the Pub, we found it full of men that stared at us as there were no women. We got the message, women were not welcome in Nova Scotia Pubs in 1960.

The next morning we made our way to the ferry to take us to Prince Edward Island with no incidents. Charlottetown is the capital so we visited the Confederation Hall where Canada became a country divided into Provinces, so we learned a little history as part of our trip.

Cavendish Beach is where we have reservations in a cottage for a week, on the northeast coast of Prince Edward Island, on the Gulf of St. Lawrence. As we are quite a bit north of Maine, we had a concern that the water would be icy cold here, but it wasn't. It was perfect for swimming, because the Gulf of St. Lawrence is warm.

The beach at Cavendish Beach is empty and spectacular in 1960 a perfect place for a vacation getaway. We enjoyed it so much reading books every day, walking the beach, swimming or just sleeping in the sunshine on a chaise lounge. Lazy yes, but we were frugal and saved a little money for a vacation each year.

Our week at Cavendish Beach was up and we decided to cross the Province of New Brunswick on our way home. The route we took paralleled the Bay Of Fundy with the highest tides in the world, so high in fact that it causes a tidal bore at Fredericton, New Brunswick. We wanted to see the tidal bore so we headed on to Fredericton where we spent the night.

The St. John's River empties into the Bay of Fundy and when the high tide comes in, it causes the river to reverse as the tidal bore rushes up the river. Quite interesting as the tide in the Bay of Fundy fluctuates more than 19 feet.

Another attraction in New Brunswick is the Longest Covered Bridge in the World that we did drive through to cross the St. John's River.

Our plan was to travel north to Madawaska the northernmost town in Maine before returning once again to Quebec City where the waiter spread the BB of spinach all over the tablecloth. Once past Madawaska we headed for the St. Lawrence River at Riviere du Loup and followed the river to the shrine at St. Ann du Baupre and finally the Statue of Samuel de Champlain adjacent to the Chateau Frontenac.

Back in Hawthorne, NJ we were thankful to be home again after such a great adventure. "What about next year", we thought. We decided to take it as it comes, as travel is cumulative and it is the combination of all these adventures that expand your mind and make you who you are.

Renting an apartment is one thing, but we really should be saving for a house. I am still pretty young and houses near the Hawthorne, Glen Rock area are pretty expensive. So all we do is look.

chapter xv

CONVENTION SPEAKER

I WRITE professional papers for my company and am accepted as a speaker at the Special Libraries Association Convention in Washington, DC. This will be an all expense vacation paid for by ITT Federal Electric Corporation. The convention hotel is the impressive Sheraton Park Hotel with Senator Hubert Humphries as the Keynote Speaker. I am to address this convention as Librarian (manager) of one of the largest technical libraries in the United States. The DEWLIne Technical Library System with 71 branch libraries.

Now I get a chance to show Jackie Washington, DC with all the monuments commemorating America's greatness.

My high school experience in public speaking to hundreds of students, almost weekly in the auditorium, has certainly prepared me for The Sheraton Park Hotel Convention Hall, where I will address thousands.

Senator Hubert Humphrey's address was better than mine, but mine was better than most. Jackie and I spent a week at the Sheraton Park Hotel seeing all the current sights of Washington, DC. We visited some favorite sights including the Lincoln Memorial, Washington Monument, Ford's Theatre, the White House, Jefferson Memorial, the Capital Building Rotunda,

Patty and her Dad

Statuary Hall, Georgetown, Arlington Cemetery, The Cathedral, and many famous restaurants. A nice adventure paid by my employer.

It did not take me long to figure out that my employer could pay for and expand my annual vacation each year if I remained creative and write a professional paper that is accepted by a convention. My earned vacation was two weeks each year and invitations to conventions typically added another week or more so my eyes were always open for new opportunities.

chapter xvi

SYSTEM DEVELOPMENT CORPORATION

COMPARING MY job to the market place caused me to respond to an ad for Information Systems Manager at System Development Corporation in the same Industrial Park in Paramus, NJ as ITT.

I was hired immediately at a salary of $6,000. per year. Thousand dollar increases were not easy in 1962 so I was elated.

System Development Corporation has been compared to the Rand Corporation, both were considered a *THINK TANK* on the west coast. My job starts with a month vacation each year and a wonderful new manager, Al Cushing, who gave me free reign to experiment, design and implement information systems.

Al liked the idea that I could write papers that were accepted by National Conventions and actually became my next mentor suggesting I write for the ADI, American Documentation Institute, fast becoming the foremost authority in the area of Information Science or more specifically Information Retrieval.

Al was at least 15 years older than me and we treated each other with the utmost respect. He saw in me a desire for greatness and individuality and encouraged me to continue on this path. He taught me that: "If you don't toot your own horn, nobody is going to toot it for you".

Under the free reign given to me by Al Cushing, I invented the SATIRE System, an information retrieval system which became a forerunner to today's internet. I wrote many professional papers on SATIRE the acronym for <u>S</u>emi <u>A</u>utomatic <u>T</u>echnical <u>I</u>nformation <u>RE</u>trieval.

My professional paper was accepted at the ADI Convention at the Diplomat Hotel in Hollywood, Florida. Jackie and I have never been to Florida, so we decided to drive and see all the east coast states on the way. Virginia, North and South Carolina, Georgia and Florida were all new to us so we really benefited from the experience.

A Florida vacation paid for my SDC at the fancy Diplomat Hotel certainly enhanced our travel repertoire. The morning of my presentation at the Diplomat Convention Center that held thousands of people interested in information retrieval. Before the meeting I met with the slide projector operator who reviewed the professional slides made for me by the SDC graphic arts department.

At age 25 I was probably the youngest person ever to address this convention . As I got to the podium the first slide appeared and it was not the proper slide, then the second slide appeared and still not correct. The entire audience was so quiet and felt my disappointment, until I proclaimed, "Fear not, apparently someone dropped the slides. However, I know my stuff and we shall have a random presentation."

As each random slide came up I discussed it in detail and tied them all together to end the presentation successfully. The audience went wild, clapping and cheering Bravo at the conclusion with many coming forward to get my business card.

Two senior executives from System Development Corporation came up to congratulate me and said, "Amazing how you held that audience in the palm of your hand." Jackie, sitting in the front row next to Peter Lund a scientist with 21 or more IBM Patents agreed and was proud of her husband.

After that presentation at the ADI Convention at the Diplomat Hotel in Hollywood, Florida the SATIRE System gained nationwide recognition. System Development Corporation ran full page ads on SATIRE in such prestigious magazines as Scientific American, Datamation, Science & Technology, . Aviation Week, etc., and more.

The boy genius, fifth grade failure has finally arrived.

I was invited often to System Development Corporation Headquarters that is located in Santa Monica, CA. to give SATIRE presentations to their west coast scientists. Each visit would last a week, and I would fly first class and stay in Santa Inez Inn in Malibu or the Miramar or Oceana Hotel in Santa Monica.

On one of my visits I was fortunate enough to walk into the Point Restaurant in Malibu and see just one person sitting at the bar who turned out to be my favorite actor in those years. I introduced myself to Charles Bronson by letting him know that as my favorite actor he was well on his way to super stardom. He laughed and asked me so many questions about Vermont that we stayed until closing. Many years later he became a reference for me introducing one of my screenplays.

The following year my professional paper was once again accepted at the ADI Convention, this time at the Pick Congress Hotel on Michigan Avenue in Chicago, IL. Once again, rather than fly, Jackie and I drove the distance from New Jersey to Chicago visiting Niagara Falls on the way.

Returning to SDC Paramus New Jersey after this convention, the upper management team met with me to inform me that I had an invitation from IBM Corporation to give a presentation to their information scientists at San Jose CA. They informed me that are very aware of the publicity I was creating for SDC and are willing to pay for this trip.

1966, Warwick NY, Michael 2, Patty, 6.

This trip gave me an opportunity to spend a week in the San Francisco Bay area and meet with many IBM employees. The effect of these meetings was to inform me that if I anticipate a career in Information Systems why not be with number one, big blue, IBM? Before I left Peter Lund and other senior executives suggested that they would like to set up an interview for me at the nearest IBM facility to where I lived.

"Nothing ventured, nothing gained" thought I, so I granted permission. A letter arrived from IBM Advanced System Development Division, Yorktown Heights, NY setting up an appointment. I was making $6,500. A year with a month vacation at SDC and IBM offered a starting salary of $12,000 with only 2 weeks vacation. I needed time to consider this offer with my mentor Al Cushing.

I showed Al my written offer from IBM and he said take it, that's what you have been working so hard for. Big blue, that's job security. ITT where you came from and SDC are both dependant on government contracts. When the contract ends your job is at risk, with IBM you will no longer be faced with contracts ending.

It was very difficult leaving the best manager I ever had, but his advice was sound. They gave me monogrammed briefcase at my going away party and wished me luck. There was not a single day I was not happy working for Al Cushing and System Development Corporation.

chapter xvii

IBM CORPORATION

IBM IS across the Hudson River on the Bear Mountain Bridge from where I lived in Warwick, NY so they certainly found the closest place for me to join the company. Even though I was paid so much, I was still quite junior to those I was working with. I was assigned to the Marketing Department to determine if putting all the laws of New York State on an information retrieval system was a viable business opportunity for IBM.

I spent most of the year in New York City's Greenwich Village at NYU Law Library with a Jewish colleague who introduced me to Katz's Delicatessen where we had many lunches. To date Katz's Deli is still my favorite. Nothing much came of this research except that we decided it was feasible.

My closest friend at IBM was Ken Schroff an MBA graduate of Harvard Business School. He and I discussed the stock market every day and with his help I invested $500.00 and turned it into $25,000.00 in a single year by investing in new issues like COMSAT, Communications Satellite Corporation.

IBM often stands for I've been moved, and so it was that I was offered a transfer to Kingston, NY a manufacturing facility making the new 360 computer. The incentive for me was that IBM would buy my house and move me for free with a raise in pay.

With this new found wealth, Jackie and I discussed the possibility of finding a way to move back to Vermont as a wonderful place to bring up children. With that in mind I decided to start a sideline business in Burlington, Vermont to increase my chances of moving to Vermont.

I hired an IBM Engineer to run the business as well as my younger brother Jimmy, now with a degree in accounting from St. Bonaventure University to keep the books for me, while I stay at IBM Kingston, NY. Operating a remote business was fun for awhile but to make a long story short, the business lasted a year and went bankrupt.

Some say you lost $25,000.00, not really, I just lost my original $500.00 investment and I learned so much about running your own business and bankruptcy that the entire experience was worth it.

chapter xviii

CRUISE SHIP EXPERIENCE

KINGSTON NY is an old river town, at one time it was the capital New York State. It was about one hour closer to Vermont where I eventually wanted to live so we rented a house and enjoyed the community. It was from Kingston that Jackie and I took advantage of the IBM Club offering a cruise to the Caribbean and Bahamas.

Jackie and Helena Philips on our first cruise.

We met Bill and Helene Philips, a very nice couple on this cruise also from IBM Kingston that made our time in Kingston, very enjoyable. We flew to Curacao in the Dutch West Indies, to board the Chandris Cruise Ship SS Regina as it sailed to Kingston, Jamaica. We spent most of the trip on deck drinking .25 cent St. Pauli Girl or Heineken beer or way down below decks in the Bazooki Room dancing to the Greek music. This trip was inexpensive on a very old Greek ship but was fun nevertheless.

Nassau and Grand Bahamas Island in the Bahamas were the last two ports, so our travels have been expanded to include the Caribbean and the Bahamas, but more important the lesson learned that cruise ships are a way to travel without the hassle of packing and unpacking, with all dining and entertainment included in complete luxury that will certainly impact our future travels.

Little did I realize at that time the impact on my life that this first cruise ship experience provided.

Our kids are growing up so fast. 1967

chapter xix

CALIFORNIA AND HAWAII

MY SISTER Carol was a flight attendant for American Airlines and one day at LAX returning from Santa Monica, we surprised each other by accidentally walking by each other in the airport. She offered to give Jackie and I a free flight to the West Coast anytime I wanted. I let her know that I sure would like to show Jackie California and decided to set up something soon.

Once I learned what Open Jaw meant in the airline industry. I put it to good use. Jackie and I planned a trip from New York to San Francisco and return from San Diego a city I desired to experience. We also booked a flight from San Francisco to Hawaii for only $199 per person round trip with a return to San Diego. Open Jaw allows you to return from a different city at no additional cost. With my sisters free tickets on American Airlines to San Francisco we left for a fantastic vacation.

We stayed at the Mark Hopkins Hotel in San Francisco and had dinner entertained by Liberace's brother George, playing the violin. We rented a car to drive to Yosemite and Sequoia National Parks. Both National Parks exceeded our expectations and totaled our National Park experience to three counting Acadia National Park in Maine.

In Hawaii we stayed at Hilton Hawaiian Village where Jackie said "I think I see Paladin having a cocktail at a nearby table". I got up and walked over and said:

"Mr. Boone, I thought I would like to mention how much I enjoy your *Repertoire Theatre* each week".

"Will you and your wife please join us as rarely do I receive such as response", he said.

"Why is that?"

"Everyone sees me as Paladin! I have to get rid of that stereotype."

We talked about his so many talents as characters he portrays on *Repertoire Theatre* and made his day.

He was a fine host and made our day as well.

We rented a car for the week and circled the Island of Oahu, saw all the sugar cane and pineapples, the high mountains with threatening storms. Visited Pearl Harbor, the Arizona Monument and finally attended a Luau before realizing there are so many old retired people here and we are still so young.

You have to do it while you can I said. We are 6000 miles from home. My sister certainly helped us afford this trip that we are both enjoying. Certainly from California it is no big deal to visit Hawaii but from the East Coast it is expensive and time consuming. You pretty much have to be retired to afford the time.

After a week in Hawaii we were ready for our first visit to San Diego. The plane lands at Lindberg Field named for Charles Lindbergh and a cab takes us to the tallest building in San Diego in 1969, the El Cortez Hotel. After taking the modern outside glass elevator to the top floor we had dinner with expansive views of this beautiful city.

Our stay in San Diego allowed us time to visit the world famous zoo, the beautiful beaches, the embarcadero, and Balboa Park.

We also rented a car in San Diego for trips to Point Loma, Pacific Beach and La Jolla. La Jolla, CA a part of San Diego is often compared to Nice, France for it's beautiful cliff walk along the breaking surf and spectacular Mediterranean climate, fine restaurants and upscale shopping.

With the Mexican Border only 15 miles from San Diego, we spent one day visiting Tijuana the closest border town in Mexico before returning to the El Cortez Hotel in San Diego.

As we board the plane to return to return to our home near Kingston, NY I say to Jackie:

"I know it is only 1969 but La Jolla or San Diego is where I would someday like to retire."

"You are only 29 and thinking about retirement, you have got to be kidding."

"I'm not, If you don't plan ahead, time will pass you by."

"Dream the ideal! Focus on your dreams, and someday you will attain it."

chapter xx
IBM HEADQUARTERS

RETURNING TO work at IBM Kingston I am given an unusual opportunity of an interview in IBM Headquarters at Armonk, New York. It seems that IBM Headquarters is looking to hire an expert in Information Retrieval to design a management information system for the Corporate Personnel Department.

My interview was with the Corporate Executive in charge and we both hit it off. He promised me that if I would leave Kingston and work for him for one year that I could be transferred to any location of my choice.

"Burlington, Vermont?" I asked.

"Of course, if that is your choice," he said.

I was pretty excited when I returned home to tell Jackie, that if I transfer to IBM Headquarters for a year with a raise and a free move that we will eventually move to IBM Burlington, VT. How ironic fate has become when you consider that I opened up a sideline business in Burlington that failed and in hindsight, it was totally unnecessary as IBM is to eventually transfer me there.

Jackie and I discussed this offer and within a week I accepted and we prepared to move to Waldwick, New Jersey where I took an option on a house. Waldwick is within 45 minutes of IBM Armonk, NY by car across the Hudson River on the Tappan Zee Bridge. Jackie was quite familiar with this part of New Jersey. We both had friends and relatives nearby from our earlier experiences in Hawthorne and Glen Rock.

chapter xxi

NEW JERSEY LIVING

RETURNING TO New Jersey for a new job at IBM Headquarters our home in Waldwick was one block from the Saddle River border. My parents for the past year are living in their new home adjacent to the northern border of Saddle River, NJ so it was an easy commute through Saddle River for mom's family gatherings.

Living so close to New York City was a wonderful experience for our children. We took them to the Museum of Natural History where they especially enjoyed the dinosaurs and the Museum of Art's Impressionist Paintings. Walking around Washington Square, visiting Central Park and dinner with the kids at Mama Leone's is something they still remember.

Jackie and I also made a point to see many Broadway Plays, starting with *Hair,* the night before opening, we both predicted it's future success. Michelle Lee stared in *How to Succeed in Business without really trying,* a nice musical and Sandy Dennis in the comedy *Any Wednesday.*

My favorite actress at that time was Lee Remick who was starring in *Wait Until Dark,* so after the performance I went to her dressing room and she cordially, with her beautiful smile gave me her autograph on Playbook.

Bill and Helena Phillips from Kingston, NY were frequent visitors to our home in Waldwick. We went together to the New York World's Fair and saw Michaelangelo's *Pieta* on loan for display. This was our second World's Fair together as Bill and Helene attended Expo 67 in Montreal with us.

John Keefe and his manager Bob working as IBM Contractors invited

Jackie and I out for my birthday for a night on the town in New York City. The plan was cocktails at *Copacabana,* dinner at the *Forvum of the Twelve Caesar's* and dancing at the *Riverboat Lounge* in the Empire State Building with an overnight stay Americana Hotel.

From 1955 to 1969 I have often been told that I am a look-a-like to Johnny Carson. After the three couples checked into the Americana we get on the elevator to start the evening and I freeze. Johnny Carson and friend are on the same elevator. Johnny stares at his look-a-like and I say nothing in shock.

Finally at the lobby, the door opens and we all depart laughing because my friends noticed the amazing resemblance. We head outside to get a cab, and my friends get a limo instead. The limo driver introduced himself as Johnny Carson's driver off duty for the evening and said he will take us anywhere we want.

"*Copacabaña* for cocktails and *Forvum of the Twelve Caesars*" was John Keefe's reply.

This evening was certainly a night to remember and remember it we will. These guys ordered three hor's d' oeuvre platters for the three couples before dinner. Awesome. For dinner I ordered Wild Boar while the others ordered exotic dinners as well.

The limo driver waited for us at each restaurant and club before returning us safely to the Americana Hotel. What a birthday! What good friends I have made at IBM HQ!

John and Bob invited Jackie and I to their homes in Westchester County for bridge night on the New York side of the Hudson River often. It is not that we let them win, they are much better bridge players than Jackie and I. The three couples had many good times together.

Business trips to Dothan Alabama where the SATIRE System was successfully installed at the Army Combat Development Command allowed me to take side trips to Huntsville Space Center for a tour of rockets and Space capsules.

Keeping up to date on Information Science on a business trip to Boston, I checked out the Impressionist collection in the Boston Museum of Art and had dinner at *Café Budapest* serenaded with Hungarian Rhapsodies. Adventure is cumulative and I started so young.

At work my close friends were Ed Zuckerman interested in art and Kathie McHale the secretary to the manager who hired me. Ed knew my interest in the Paul Chabas painting *September Morn* and let me know that if I ever find a suitable reproduction, he will frame it in the art gallery where he works part time.

I needed a female opinion so on our lunch hour Kathie and I set out to find this painting in White Plains, NY. I was hoping Kathie would advise me that even if nude that it is a work of art in good taste.

Kathie agreed so I had it mounted and gave it to Ed for framing. The 1912 painting won the Medal of Honor at the Paris Salon and became scandalous when displayed in a New York Gallery in 1913 with attempts to ban it in the United States.

Ed had two reasonable priced frames, one perfect but ugly the other spectacular in green and gold that doesn't fit requiring the painting to be trimmed. So I slightly trimmed the right side. The painting depicts a nude female in soft pink standing in a lake tastefully composed against a grey background. Ed's frame sets it off beautifully.

Once home the painting is hung over the fireplace and a few days later Jackie told me that Michael wants to show his little friends his Dad's Chabas so they all march in to look. Ha!

Kids! Aren't they fun?

Dad's Chabas.

More of a coincidence is that on a later visit to the Metropolitan Museum of Art as we enter to see our favorites we are stunned to see the original "SEPTEMBER MORN" hanging in the entrance foyer as it was in Russia and France for many years and returned to the United States in 1957 where it was no longer considered offensive but representative of 20th Century French Art.

Lunch at the *Russian Tea Room* and dinner of sauerbraten at *Luchow's* made another complete day in New York City.

One afternoon I noticed a new Corsair Sailboat in a boat dealers yard, and pulled over to inspect it with Jackie. We climbed aboard and realized that it slept four people that I thought might be ample for our family.

"Someday I would like a boat like this, Jackie. What do you think?"

"It would be nice, but there is so much we have to do first."

"Yes a roof over your head is pretty important, but I have given a lot of thought concerning the real value of material things, many of which, other than their antique value, you would not even want today."

"Like what?"

"Take the evolution of the washing machine, from the scrub board, to the wringer washer to the modern multiple cycle washing machine. Today no would want a scrub board or a wringer washing machine, they have all been sent to the dump."

Jackie in Pumpkin Patch, Saddle River, NJ

"I guess, so what's your point?"

"There are two material things that I value very much, The sailboat and the fireplace. The sailboat has lasted thousands of years since the Phoenicians and Egyptians used them in the Mediterranean and the fireplace even longer from pre-historic times starting as a place for fire inside a cave or outside in a pit and evolved to the 1700s as a hearth and place to cook. Both defy comparison in outlasting today's materialism."

Michael and Patty with our friends
John and Kathie Derby.

"What do you call today's materialism?"

"James Michener in his book *Hawaii* when discussing the Chinese, points out how frugal they are compared to Americans who spend so much of their earned income on cars, that end up in a junk yard and are eventually crushed into small packages for recycling."

All these years, I have been motivated by Atlas Shrugged to be a known as an idealistic producer and I am only now beginning to explore the artistic side of my life. I wrote a poem called *The Purpose of Life* and have just finished reading Hemingway's *Moveable Feast* which was published posthumously by his family and it has caused me to question the direction in my life and more important the purpose of life itself.

Living in New Jersey so close to New York City was exciting but my job was getting boring so it's time to change direction and pursue that promised move to Vermont.

Was idealism the right path for me to take. If you don't like something, change it. I guess I'm pretty good at that, so it's time for Vermont, that in my mind is an ideal place to bring up children.

We took the kids to the Bronx Zoo

Our Home at 50 Campbell St., Waldwick NJ

chapter xxii

MALLETTS BAY, COLCHESTER, VERMONT

WITH A transfer to IBM Burlington, VT, we have succeeded in our quest. I quickly bought a four bedroom home within two blocks of Lake Champlain and moved the family in before Christmas. Jackie has five brothers and four sisters and many relatives living nearby.

I travel to work with no traffic lights and no traffic, just cows. In fact in 1970 there are still more cows than people in Vermont. My kid's have experienced New Jersey and even New York City so now it is time for the country life.

My Manager at IBM is a wonderful manager once again giving me free reign to be creative.

Our friends Bill and Helena Phillips from Kingston and John and Kathie Derby from Westchester plan visits to our new home in Vermont, so life is good.

Jackie and I saw our first Opera *The Barber of Seville*, sung in English. What a disaster, it was awful. We both decided against opera and I mistakenly stayed away for twenty years. Later in life I realized how important it is to carefully select your first opera.

Montreal is only 90 miles away, so some of our early activities include hockey games at the Forum where I saw Canadians vs. Boston Bruins and got Jean Belevau's autograph. The New York Giants played a pre-season exhibition game against the Pittsburg Steelers at Jarre Park in Montreal. The Giants lost and fired coach Allie Sherman not realizing we were all witnessing the start of the Pittsburg Steelers dynasty.

In Burlington we saw Edgar Lee Masters wonderful drama *Spoon River Anthology* and at University of Vermont's Theatre in the Round Shakespeare's *King Lear*.

It didn't take us long to get involved in the sports and cultural activities of the Burlington, Vermont area. Jackie and I saw many St. Michael College Basketball games and a few University of Vermont hockey games. With Lake Champlain awaiting us I signed up for the Power Squadron to learn the boating rules of the road.

chapter xxiii

ARCHITECTURE

IN MOVING from New Jersey to Vermont, my objective was to get my family settled as quickly as possible so within the first week I had already purchased a house that allowed us to have a home base where I could seek out the ideal home site.

During the first year we looked at many mountain top view lots because I had in mind to design a contemporary home with lots of glass to let the spectacular Vermont views in. Mountain top acreages were typically remote and Jackie convinced me that we should limit our search to close to home near the Colchester School system for the children.

With close to home the new requirement I noticed what could possibly be a building lot on a cliff right across the street. "Impossible"! I thought. I crossed the street walked across a neighbor's property and climbed the cliff. I stood on the cliff and could see Lake Champlain and thought if only this cliff were higher I could see more of the lake.

I climbed a tree to raise myself about 16 feet and the view became spectacular with Malletts Bay, Lake Champlain glistening below both Mt. Mansfield and Camels Hump of the Green Mountain Range. Wow! Wait until I tell Jackie what I found, like right across the street. Who-da-thunk-it!

A visit to the Colchester Town Clerk gave me the owner's name and map of the acreage. I contacted the owner who planned to build on that property himself someday and was told that the property is not for sale.

Not taking no for an answer, I immediately started to design my dream house for a family of four. I started with the 32 foot living room that for purposes of the view would be on the second story. Below it I put a 32 foot family room, knowing that at a minimum the living room floor would be at least 17 feet higher than the cliff.

Each of the 12 rooms were designed individually for maximum function and put together to form the 4000 square foot dream house.

At IBM I was promoted to Manager, Laboratory Information Systems, and was enjoying a interesting productive career.

We enrolled the kids in ski lessons first for a week at Stowe and the second year for a week at Sugarbush. The ski country is a mecca for contemporary alpine homes where I became cognizant of new ideas, some of which I incorporated in my own design. The crow's nest for example, would allow even more height for more expansive views and become my art studio.

Out of the blue I received a telephone call from the owner of the property that captured my interest. He told me he is a bachelor and would now consider selling as he had plans to travel. We agreed on a price that was more than he paid for it and both of us left the meeting happy.

Now with ownership of the land behind me, I became the Prime Contractor and negotiated deals for all the appliances at cost and started looking at siding and glass. Bill Holbrook a successful contractor in his own right was watching every move I made and when he saw the plans for my home he wanted to build it.

Bill stopped by almost daily to give me free advice. He told me I would have to blast through solid rock more than six feet down along the 100 yard driveway for the water line from the street to the house, to prevent the pipes from freezing in winter. Of course Bill was right so I hired a dynamite firm.

About a week later the noise was like World War II and the earth was shaking and Bill who could hear the noise from his house over a mile away, drove up in his Jeep and said this is over your head, I'll take it from here. He apparently resigned himself, that I am the contractor and he is the builder, another relationship that will last a lifetime.

Bill Holbrook and I became best pals. He fell in love with the project and dedicated himself to building the finest home he ever built. He knew as an IBMer I had no business to be playing with dynamite with all the neighbors angry with me, so he just assumed responsibility and I gave him free reign. He loved the project and I knew from his friendship that he was not about to rip me off.

The acreage was wooded and I decided to leave every possible tree standing and cleared only the area for the foundation and driveway. Bill showed up every morning and I was out there before work to discuss with him the days activity.

One morning he said, "You know John, I will have to step the foundation to follow the contour of the cliff which will give you a basement creating still another level and add nine feet more height to your home. Do you really need that art studio that will make this home four stories high?

"Yes Bill. go for it, now even the lower level rec room level will have great views and the giant trees around the house will conceal its size and it will surely blend in with the wooded environment using just redwood, glass and stone."

As the construction progressed, Bill had many visitors, mostly contractors like himself who were generally interested in what Bill considered his masterpiece.

chapter xxiv

KIDS PARTICIPATE

About 26 miles south of Burlington is the small town of Panton, Vermont. It was in in the open fields of Panton that grey weathered stone was laying on top of the ground for centuries so the family decided on Panton-stone for the fireplace.

For many weekends Patty and Michael and I went Panton to pick out stones laying on top of the ground that had horizontal lines from weathering over the years. It became a family project and the pile of stones at the home site kept getting larger and larger.

When Bill saw the Panton-stone he said. "I know the best craftsman to build your fireplace, but I warn you, he is temperamental and drinks a lot. He may walk off the job half finished, but he is the best."

"Bring him on Bill, between the two of us, we will try to make him happy enough to finish the job."

As the construction neared completion the outside of the home is all glass and vertical heart redwood, and the centerpiece of the interior is the spectacular grey Panton-stone fireplace built by a true artist rising from the foundation in the basement through the family room where it is very wide, then up through the living room level and loft level where it is normal size then past the art studio and outside through the roof.

Our fireplace artist only walked off the job twice but each time returned to admire his own work and finally finished the job.

Living room fireplace

Entrance Foyer and the back of Fireplaces.

Family photo in front of lower level fireplace.

Landscaping was quite easy as I left all the trees standing except for the curved driveway so you could not see the front of house from the road, only the rear and side from the road below the cliff. Not a single blade of grass to be found anywhere! An ideal, accomplished.

Michael and Snoopy in the driveway.

Patty is growing up so fast.

The front entrance.

Mike on the front deck.

In Memoriam. My sister Carol and I are all that's left in 2012.
James Roach passed at age 33, Alberta Roach 93, John P. Roach Sr. 92
Photo taken on our side deck,

Lake Champlain from our Bedroom Deck.

Dream home completed in 1972
15 Cedar Ridge Drive, Colchester, Vermont

chapter xxv
SAILING

OUR VACATIONS each year centered around the kids for they loved camping. We bought a tent and all the camping equipment needed and did Vermont State Parks during the summer. As the kids grew older we took longer vacations camping for a week at such places as Orchard Beach Maine, Cape Cod National Seashore and Exeter, New Hampshire.

While spending a quiet evening in The Dream Home.

"What are you reading, John?"

"A book on retirement."

"You're still in your thirties, don't you think it is a little early?"

"No Jackie. It says here, people die in retirement early because they don't have a hobby to keep them busy. They should start a hobby that makes money in retirement."

"Well, you do oil paintings."

"I really need a hobby that makes me grow that can make some money in retirement. Do you remember when we were first married and lived in New Jersey and I showed you a sailboat that could sleep four?"

"Yes, I remember," says Jackie..

"At that time you really had no interest and suggested that we wait until we have our house."

"Yes".

"Well we have owned three houses since then and I don't think I will ever want one nicer than this one. So now it is time for the sailboat, unless of course there is something that you want that I haven't bought for you yet."

"No. I don't think so," says Jackie. "I won't sail on it!

"Well the kids will love it. Look how many times we have taken them camping in tents at Maine, Vermont, New Hampshire and Cape Cod Campsites. Now I can take them for a weekend cruise."

"You don't know how to sail do you?"

"No, but I will in six weeks, I just enrolled in sailing lessons at Fisher's Landing in Charlotte.

"What's in the bag?"

"Well I want to buy that sailboat that I always wanted. So you have to start someplace."

He opens the bag.

"Voila! Boat shoes."

"When do you start lessons?"

"Tomorrow, after work. Two nights a week for six weeks. I will be done by July 15th. Would you like to take lessons with me?

"No. You go, maybe you can teach me."

In mid July, John's first boat is delivered, a 24 foot Sloop which sleeps four comfortably. The kids loved it but Jackie refused to go for a sail. She claimed she was afraid when it heeled over.

Didn't take my kids long, they loved it. Our tenting days are over and we loved that part of our lives, now the new adventure of exploring Lake Champlain by sailboat. The Lake is 120 miles long with the Green Mountain range on the Vermont side and Adirondack Mountains on the New York side creating awesome scenery with many coves and bays included in its 570 miles of shoreline.

The family became members of the Malletts Bay Boat Club at the end of our street. The club provided tender service to our boat moored there. Both kids were enrolled in sailing lessons at the club as well.

My work at IBM continued to be enjoyable, I eventually had an assignment that would allow me to travel to investigate computer problems anywhere, allowing me to combine business with adventure. Trips to New Orleans, Kansas City, Dallas, and even Tampa where

Patty, Mike and I learned to sail this yacht as a team.

86

I visited John and Kathie Derby's new home that expanded my travel horizons.

I met a Jean Claude, an engineer from IBM Paris, France while he was working at IBM Burlington and saw that he was lonely so I invited him to an American cook-out on our deck. Jackie prepared the baked potato, corn on the cob and salad and laid out the porterhouse steaks for Jean Claude and I to grill. He couldn't stop smiling and was amazed at how casually Americans live. He cooked his own steak to his own taste.

After dinner I took Jean Claude out sailing with the kids on Lake Champlain and he thoroughly enjoyed visiting an American family.

I took some art lessons where the teacher played Rimsky-Korsakov's *Scheherazade* constantly to inspire painters to be creative. Most of my paintings were in oils, some using a palate knife. I finished many artworks in the crows nest atop our home with the inspirational music of Rimsky-Korsakov. Later in life my book on Rimsky-Korsakov was published as, *The Mighty Kuchka*.[1]

Patty also became proficient in oil painting and completed some accomplished works. Her painting *The Sailboat Race* hangs in our living room.

We took the kids to Kennebunkport, Maine for a visit to the Maine Coast.

Mike informed me that he rather not eat at MacDonald's anymore and henceforth will always prefer Lobster to a big Mac. It's my fault for introducing him to Lobster at such a young age. Sometimes parents do the dumbest things. Feeding Mike will now cost me big.

It was during this period that I incorporated a business called Bay Harbor Yachts, Ltd. To start a sideline business that might be useful in retirement. I ordered a 29 foot Yacht and planned to sell my current boat by the time it arrived.

Members of *The Ethan Allen Club,* a prestigious gentlemen's club in Burlington invited me to join them which gave me camaraderie with the business men in the area and more contacts for introducing my new business. Although the Ethan Allen Club was during these years a men's only club, it was open for women guests every weekend and many holidays for some of the best dining in Burlington, Vermont. Jackie and I were frequent attendees.

---

1   Roach, John P. Jr., *The Mighty Kuchka*. 2009. Author House, Bloomington, IN.

chapter xxvi

EUROPE

It was a nice surprise when I came home and told Jackie that I have an IBM Business Trip to Europe.

"What for", she asked.

I am writing a paper on Palladium Depletion which is causing some failures on computers caused by sulfur contamination as at the computer in Solothurn Switzerland. So I will visit the site to determine the cause.

"Switzerland, that sounds like your horizons are expanded again."

"You are going too."

"You are taking me?"

"Of course, some of my visits will only take a few hours and the rest of the time we will see some of Europe."

"Where else?'

"We fly to Paris, France and stay for a week, then a weekend in Switzerland followed by still another week in Germany followed by a weekend any where we want."

"I know where you want to go on the last weekend."

"Where"?

You told me that after reading Michener's book, "*The Drifters*, that you would like to see for yourself the life styles of Torremelinos, Spain and swim at the Mediterranean Beaches called Costa del Sol.

"Would you like that Jackie?"

"Sure I would, when do we leave?"

"In two weeks out of Montreal on Air France."

"I'll start packing, I'm excited," said Jackie.

About 10 days letter we received a telegram from France, inviting us to dinner at Jean Claude's apartment in Paris. I showed the letter to my boss at work and he was impressed. He had been to France often and never had such an invitation. He told me, I should be honored to be so fortunate, because the French seem to be very private people.

chapter xxvii

PARIS

RATHER THAN stay at American Style Hotel where English is spoken we chose the Hotel Gare de Lyon a French hotel to experience total immersion for an entire week. Jackie speaks French a lot better than I do, so this hotel was fine. The hotel is right across the square from the namesake Lyon Train Station which is handy for my trip to the IBM plant is Essonnes, France about 40 miles south of Paris where I am scheduled to spend a day.

First we learned how to use the metro and admired the architecture of each station. I visited IBM Paris Headquarters to pay my respects where they recommended some of their finest restaurants and we did many.

Au Pied de Cochon (At the foot of the Pig) was clearly our favorite. As you approach this place near the Paris Opera at 6 Rue Coquilliere, there is a squealing pig tied to a fire hydrant, as the restaurant specializes in pigs feet. Once inside the décor is beautiful and a full French Cuisine menu is available.

We learned about the Parisian breakfast, Croissant and Coffee and repeated it every morning. No wonder Parisian men look so trim.

Spent one morning in the Louvre, built by Napoleon Bonaparte containing so many works of art including the Winged Victory dating from 2 BC and Mona Lisa watching you with those soft eyes.

The highlight for me was the Jeu de Paume (Gatehouse) where the Impressionists hung their art in defiance of Salon Judges at the Louvre. I stood there stunned seeing my favorite painting *Absinthe* by Edgar Degas, a scandalous painting in its day and his sculpture Little Dancer Age 14 (La Petite Dancer la quartorze ans).

Jackie and I saw the many Manet's, Cassatt's, Monet's, Renoir's, Gauguin's, Cezanne's, Morisot's, and the rest of the Impressionists who's works have since been moved to a larger venue at Musee d'Orsey a former train station.

Walking along the Seine River at night and buying street corner crapes and pomme frits was still another new experience for us.

Of course we went to the top of the Eiffel Tower and enjoyed the expansive views of Paris, then walked the Champs Elysses from the Arch de Triumph to Place de Concorde where the monarchy was guillotined during the revolution. People watching in the outdoor Café's along the Champs Elysses was a favorite pastime of ours while nursing a cold Fischer's Beer.

Jackie in Paris

On Thursday evening we went to Jean Claude's apartment where his wife prepared a five course French Dinner with Hor's d' Oeuvres cocktails and champagne. They started with salad and they served Veal Chops to perfection and ended with fromage, desert and coffee and brandy in such an elegant manner that Jackie and I were amazed.

Jean Caude explained to us, that in Paris apartments are small, expensive and in high demand, but if we came in the winter, he and his wife own a Castle in Chamonix ski country where he likes to entertain guests with a lot more space. We laughed as we were so thankful to be so comfortable with such nice friends.

Jackie and I finally took that trip to IBM Essonnes 40 miles south to meet Jean Claude again at work where he introduced us to many people and took us to lunch in the IBM Cafeteria where to our surprise, wine is served. The round trip train through the countryside was pleasant.

On our last full day in Paris we took the metro as far as it went toward Versailles and visited this beautiful place that triggered the French Revolution as the monarchy lived in such opulence and excess. The manicured gardens of Versailles are beautiful, the Hall of Mirrors with chandeliers repeating to infinity, excessive and the much quoted revolutionary theme, "But they have no bread? Let them eat cake!" Probably not true, but great folklore nonetheless.

Palace of Versailles

chapter xxviii
SWITZERLAND

I REMEMBER Jackie not feeling well as we boarded Swiss Air for Switzerland. We landed at Zurich and rented a car. I was worried that Jackie might have the flu so we headed for Interlaken to start climbing the Alps to a Chalet that I had rented in Grindelwald high in the Alps to let Jackie recuperate with a nap.

A few hours later she woke up went out on the deck, admired the alpine scenery and said she was fully recovered with all this fresh air and sunshine so high in the Alps.

"What's for dinner", Jackie asked.

"How about cocktails and Swiss Fondue"?

Grindelwald, Switzerland

The next morning we headed for Jungfrau (Young Virgin) from Grindelwald by cog railway destined for Jungfraujoch the highest train station in Europe at 11,322 feet. The cog railway trip allowed us to see the many hundreds of chalets and farms amidst the granite walls of Jungfrau rising 13,642 feet with the *Sphinx Observatory* and observation platform accessible by elevator from the train station also referred to as the *Top of Europe,* with views to France, Germany and Austria.

Another highlight of this cog railway trip is the Ice Palace at Jungfraujoch defined as a castle carved out of ice that people can walk through hallways leading to many rooms containing ice sculptures. Sure it is cold, but Jackie and I really did enjoy the experience.

Jackie at the entrance to the Ice Palace, Jungfrau, Switzerland

Returning to Grindelwald going down hill on the cog railway through all the tunnels was just as much fun as the start of the trip. This day at *The Top of Europe* was an experience we shall never forget.

I still had a responsibility to determine where the sulfur contamination was coming from in a Bank in Solothurn so on Monday morning Jackie and I checked out of the Chalet and headed for this small town where to my disbelief was a fertilized roof garden on the floor above the computer room. Sulfur from the fertilizer provided the contamination.

Jackie and I toured Lake Lucerne and with lunch in Zurich before our Lufthansa flight to Stuttgart, Germany.

chapter xxix

GERMANY

WE ARE scheduled to spend a week in Germany that will start in Stuttgart where IBM has a nearby laboratory. Rather than stay in an American Hotel we once again chose an ethnic German Hotel as the best way to experience the German people and customs. Language was not a problem as English has by 1973 become the language of technology and most people in Germany are already bi-lingual.

I rented a BMW for my stay in Stuttgart because after my visit to the IBM facility we intended to visit the Black Forest of Germany, home of so many different types of Cuckoo Clocks. The Black Forest, so named from the darkness provided by canopies of massive numbers of trees blocking the sunlight. Pines and firs dominate the landscape.

Black Forest, Germany

The Black Forest is composed of many small villages as well, where we sampled locally made sausage platters with a stein of German Beer.

After a full day of touring the Black Forest we returned to our hotel in Stuttgart for one of my favorite dinners of Sauerbraten, potato dumplings and Jackie likes it with red cabbage.

Stuttgart also has the landmark Fernsatrum, a TV Tower with a

Castle in Black Forest, Germany

restaurant near the top, that we of course made a point to dine with views of the entire city.

We spent so much time driving around the Black Forest villages that only have a few days left in Germany and I have appointments at IBM Mainz and IBM Hannover, so we drove to Frankfort and stayed at the Mainz Hilton on the edge of the Rhine River.

I left Jackie at the Mainz Hilton with wonderful views of the river traffic on the Rhine, while I completed business at IBM.

The next day we spent some time driving around Frankfort before

The Fernsatrum, Stuttgart, Germany

turning in the BMW at the Train Station awaiting still another new experience. An overnight first class cabin on a European Sleeping Car for our trip from Frankfort to Hannover. The clickety- click of the train just lulled me to sleep. Breakfast in the dining car as we pulled into Hannover.

Hannover is a very modern city as it was completely destroyed in World War II by bombing runs from England, so I am told there was nothing left over 3 feet high. Since the war Hannover has been completely rebuilt. With the weekend approaching I finished my IBM Business and we flew to Madrid.

chapter xxx
SPAIN

WE LANDED in Madrid, which gave us to opportunity to tour the city and visit the Prado Gallery considered one of the world's finest Art Museums. We saw the great works of El Greco, Valazquez and Francisco de Goya. Goya's famous *La Maya Vestida* and *La Maya Desnuda* were both on display showing the legendary *Duchess of Alba,* both clothed and nude. Experts even today argue if the face was added to both bodies. Regardless, it's art!

Madrid, Spain

Later in the day we went to a Spanish Restaurant in Madrid for fish and I had never seen completely round French fries with a hole in the middle. I stared at these things until I reasoned that they must be sliced and hollowed out squid, so I asked the waiter.

"Calamari" the waiter said.

Well, no wonder in 1973 I had yet to see Calamari on any menu in the US, but no doubt it will be here soon as it was delicious.

I've always used squid for bait going deep sea fishing and now I ate it.

It was only a short flight from Madrid to Malaga, where I rented the smallest car I ever saw for our trip to nearby Torremelonos. This car was so small that our luggage hardly fit.

This time we wanted an American Hotel, because my Spanish is lacking so we stayed at the Torremelinos Holiday Inn Beachfront. With three days here we were very comfortable as Jackie and I loved swimming for the first time in the Mediterranean.

Jackie in the sun, Holiday Inn Beach Front, Torremelinos, Spain

Torremelinos, Spain was everything I expected. Fun people, good food, beautiful beaches on the Costa del Sol (coast of the sun) and even an evening Gaucho Dinner at El Retamar in nearby Malaga.

We did so much in these two weeks on our first trip to Europe and we have a long flight from Malaga to New York then from New York to Burlington, VT that will give us time to reflect on so many new experiences.

chapter xxxi
ROCINANTE

Accused of being too idealistic and a hopeless romantic since my high school days I saw no reason not to admit it.

Our new 29 foot Yacht has arrived and is named "Rocinante" after Don Quixote's horse. In Cervantes's book, Rocinante was not a speedy thoroughbred, but rather a clumsy farm horse.

Chosen by the idealist Don Quixote as his stead to slay windmills in defense of women's purity, Rocinante only added to the vision of a crazy old man in his golden helmet atop a large horse ready to defend his ideal woman Dulcinea. (Sp. sweetheart, beloved of Don Quixote).

When I told Patty the story of Don Quixote and played the music of *Man of La Mancha* on our stereo for her, she cried. So I hugged her until she stopped, knowing that my daughter understands.

Patty saw the connection between idealism and Rocinante and offered to paint the transom of our new Yacht. I agreed and Patty went to work as she has a lot of talent.

When the transom was finished, I was amazed. It is a beautiful picture of Don Quixote on Rocinante galloping in a charge with his lance forward toward nothing but you know there must be windmills in the distance..

What a daughter! What talent!

Thanks, Patty!

Rocinante painted in gold on both sides as well.

Family sailing on Rocinante, Patty at the bow, Michael at the Helm, Mom and Dad relaxing..

Mike letting his Dad relax.

Lake Champlain from our deck.

chapter xxxii

TORTOLA

SIX MONTHS later while on our winter vacation in Tortola, British Virgin Islands, we are sitting at lunch having pina coladas, when a young couple comes in and can't find a table.

"Join us if you like."

"Thank you, I'm Joan and this is my husband Bob."

"Hi, this is my wife Jackie and my name is John."

A Waitress comes over and takes their order.

"What brings you to Tortola?" inquires Joan.

"My company sent me on a business trip to St. Croix, so we decided to take an extra week and spend it here and visit St. John and St. Thomas. I think I made a mistake though."

"How?"

"I had no idea Tortola would be this beautiful or this Long Bay Resort so fantastic. I will hate to go to St. Thomas after this."

Bob says, "How long can you stay here with us?"

"Five more days here then two days in St.Thomas. What do you do for work Bob?"

"I really don't have to work, but I am trained as an architect. Joan works. She is a ballerina for a Ballet Co. in New York.

"Wow. Pretty good Joan. How did you do that?"

"You just put your mind to it Jackie. I was a high paid advertising executive on Madison Avenue. At night I took ballet lessons and finally quit to do what I wanted to do with my life."

"All we have is our life span, you might as well do with it, that which you enjoy most," says John.

"John, do you like your job."

"Yes this year I do Joan, I have a great boss and a great job, but that won't last forever."

"Why do you say that?"

"I have already been with the Company 11 years. Only two years were rewarding and fantastic the other nine years were a waste of my life."

"What would you like to do?"

"Establish my own business in Yacht Sales."

"You are a sailor?" Bob asks.

"Yes, I had a 24 foot sloop last summer and now a 29 footer that was just delivered."

"So, you are already in business?" remarks Bob.

"At his point it is only a sideline for retirement."

Joan points out to sea:

"Look at all those yachts here sailing into the coves. Next year I would like to come here again and charter a boat. John, will you teach us how to sail?

"I would love to. Tortola is a sailors Paradise."

*My brother Jimmy, (James T. Roach),
teaching customer how to rig a sailboat.*

During the last day on the beach in Tortola. Bob, Joan, Jackie and John have been inseparable all week. Bob is scuba diving with his mask nearby and Jackie is getting four pina coladas. John and Joan are sitting together on the beach.

"Will you really come back next winter and charter a boat with us and teach us to sail?

"Of course. In fact I will teach you to sail on Lake Champlain. You and Bob can visit Vermont next summer and we will put you up for as long as you like."

"Oh! That would be great."

"Bob as an architect would like our house, as I designed it myself and it is like no other house. It is contemporary and all glass, redwood and stone on a cliff overlooking Lake Champlain."

"Bob would like that."

Jackie approaches with a tray of pina coladas.

"Here are your drinks."

"Thanks Jackie," says Joan.

"I just invited Bob and Joan to Vermont next summer."

"That's great John."

"Come visit us too, we have a house on Long Island which has been photographed for one of the House Beautiful type Magazines, and an apartment in Greenwich Village which we use every day when I go to work."

"Great! I know Greenwich Village very well as I did some work for IBM at New York University in the village, so it will be fun to visit you both.

Pristine Cane Garden Bay, Tortola, as it was in 1974

We spent the first vacation exploring Tortola with Joan and Bob on land and returned again the next year to charter a fully provisioned Out Island 41 Ketch, big enough for three couples to share in separate cabins.

Morgan Out Island 41 Chartered Yacht, anchored at Cane Garden Bay, Tortola.

Jackie and Joan Bailey enjoying a full week on a provisioned, chartered yacht.

110

Bob and Joan Bob Bailey visited our home in Vermont where we introduced them to Ed and Linda Murphy who would become the third

Long Bay, Tortola

couple on our upcoming planned vacation in Tortola again. We took Joan and Bob out sailing on Lake Champlain and taught them the where the wind is at all times and how to handle a yacht.

All three couples were now ready and eager to depart from Roadtown Harbor, Tortola an a fully provisioned yacht for a week in the British Virgin Islands.

We anchored off many islands and rowed the dingy ashore to check them out. The women on board made sure we had cocktails and hor's d'Oeuvres at sundown before a fine dining that they prepared in the galley. Sometimes the men prepared steaks on the barbecue that overhung the stern. There was plenty of beer and wine every day while sailing.

Some of the highlight visits were the famous *Baths* of Virgin Gorda, where unusual rocks set up cave-like structures containing crystal clear water for swimming. In Virgin Gorda we also anchored overnight in Little Dix Bay and enjoyed some shore activities.

By now all three couples were on sailor time. At sunrise, everyone is ready for breakfast and by sundown preparing to asleep. Sailing is great exercise out in the sunshine and fresh air so when the sun sets, you are tired.

We were planning to go to *Foxy's* on the island of Jost Van Dyke. We anchored out and went ashore in the dingy and found *Foxy's* closed for a week so we returned to the yacht to prepare dinner. A small power boat pulled up and the driver asked if we would like a local home cooked Jost Van Dyke meal prepared by his wife.

Didn't take us long to accept as we all got into his power boat and headed to his home on the island. Jost Van Dyke at the time had no electricity, so once again the family lived from sun up to sun down. The host and his wife prepared a nice dinner of local fish that we enjoyed. After dinner the host provided local entertainment by teaching us how to play dominoes. In this manner we did experience Jost Van Dyke hospitality.

After such a nice evening with our host we cast off in the morning for Cane Garden Bay, Tortola. This Bay is protected by coral reefs and is one of the most beautiful anchorages in Tortola. The beach is pristine and contains a shack called *Stanley's* that serves lobster. We did meet Stanley who is quite the entrepreneur, as he also runs the school bus which is an open truck with lots of seats for the happy smiling kids as well as other small businesses.

We are on the windward side of Tortola at the protected Cane Garden Bay behind a reef for a good nights sleep and are thinking on anchoring off unprotected Long Bay in the morning. We did anchor off Long Bay, enjoyed their resort but didn't stay long as the wind was coming up .

We set sail and traversed the narrows between St. John and Tortola to once again be on the leeward side of Tortola. With our week charter just about over and our provisions getting low we had one more night to enjoy. Bound for Norman Island that contains a very modern Rocky Resort, we entered their tiny harbor and dropped anchor.

What a way to end a week of sailing, in a fancy resort, with dinner, music and dancing. We knew it was our last evening with the yacht so we stayed up late and enjoyed the festivities. To date, I would have to say that this vacation will be remembered a lifetime.

We returned the yacht in Roadtown before noon and said good by to Linda and Ed who returned to Burlington while Bob and Joan joined us for a few more days at Long Bay Resort.

Tortola under sail ranks as one of our best vacations.

chapter xxxiv

A FATHER ONLY

I WOULD make no sense to discuss the reasons why, but in 1975 I filed for separation and divorce from Jackie in the State of Vermont. Having found the courage to no longer be a husband, the only issue remaining is how can I be a good father to my two children that I love so very much.

Only time will tell if I succeeded.

My first and most important objective is to make sure my children understand that I am not leaving them. That my Bay Harbor Yachts office is only two blocks away overlooking Malletts Bay, Lake Champlain and I expect them to visit often and at any time they choose.

At the time I was taking Mike for his bowling league every Saturday morning. There will be no change, I will continue every Saturday to pick him up for bowling for as long as he wishes. Patty wanted Ballet lessons and tried for awhile

Might be a strike, Mike?

knowing that whatever she wanted I would be there to encourage her. I picked her up and took her to ballet lessons but she eventually got into horses and was quite happy.

Both kids were enrolled in sailing lessons at the Malletts Bay Boat Club next door to my business, so they would visit realizing their Dad did not leave them. Michael made a point to ride his bike to see me every day while Patty, so much under her mother's influence needed more time to realize her Dad is not a bad person that he was made out to be.

Divorce in Vermont in 1976 was almost unheard of. Vermont was not a community property state and had antiquated divorce laws. People tended to stay married in a dysfunctional marriage to avoid the hassle of divorce, but an idealist would not.

In 1975 I took a second wife in a spiritual marriage with vows before God as described in the book *Serial Monogamy* published in 2011. I loved her very much until the day she died of cancer.

I married a third time to Micheline Tremblay, a French Teacher from Montreal, Canada on four yachts rafted together in Malletts Bay and left on a honeymoon in the Greek Islands.

Wedding with more than 50 guests many from New Jersey and Vermont

Wedding Ceremony

Micheline on our honeymoon in Mykonos, Greece.

Mykonos, Greece, so good, I will visit again.

Of course we spent some time in Athens, saw the Acropolis, Parthenon, Temple of Apollo, rented a car and drove out to Sounion to visit the Temple of Poseidon, visited the amphitheatre at Epidaurus and the hand dug Corinth Canal, but Mykonos was definitely a very special place with its maze of alleys, white buildings and windmills and certainly a place to visit again.

Did I say windmills? If only Rocinante was here, I am sure I could find a lance.

chapter xxxiv
LAKE CHAMPLAIN CRUISE

I HAVE taken the kids sailing in the northern part of lake Champlain often to places like Valcour Island and Burton Island for a weekend, but the southern part of the Lake has more spectacular scenery of Vermont's Green Mountain Range to the east and the Adirondacks to the west in New York State.

Micheline and I took the kids for a full week cruise on Lake Champlain. Since my college days I was fascinated by the folk lore and history of Lake Champlain and knew down deep that I would eventually write a book on the subject which I did later in life in the year 2007 titled *The Fourteenth State*. 2.

The kids and I provisioned the yacht and planned a trip all the way to historic Fort Ticonderoga, the keystone fortress at the very narrow part of the water highway, Lake Champlain, preventing the British in Montreal from joining the British in New York during the Revolutionary war in 1776.

So many historic sites to see and two eager kids to learn the history of their state. The first day we sailed out of Malletts Bay bound for our mooring in Shelburne Bay, took the dingy ashore and had dinner at our favorite French Restaurant, Café Shelburne.

At dinner that night the kids asked for the story of Ft. Ticonderoga considered the Gibraltar of the 13 Colonies guarding the narrow passage on the water highway, between Canada and New York City. So here is an excerpt from my book, *The Fourteenth State*:

May 10, 1775. Ethan's captains arrive at Hand's Cove with their companies.

A lone horseman in a red coat arrives on a speeding horse, which rears on its hind legs and stops as the rider jumps off in front of Captain Remember Baker, who grabs the reins.

"Whoa! Where do you think you are going?"

"I am Major Benedict Arnold of the Connecticut Foot Guards. I have been sent to command troops to take Fort Ticonderoga."

"Hogwash! We follow no one but Ethan Allen."

"I am now in command to take the fort," says Arnold.

"Where are your troops, then?"

"I have none. I am here to command these troops."

"Seth, tell this perfumed foot guard what his chances are."

"We follow no one but Ethan Allen. Here he comes now!"

A large white horse enters the glen with Ethan Allen in full uniform, who asks,

"Who is this Redcoat?"

"I am Major Arnold of the Connecticut Foot Guard, sent to command these troops to take Fort Ticonderoga."

Authoritatively Ethan replies,

"Well, I am Commandant COLONEL Ethan Allen, commander of the Green Mountain Boys. Considering you have brought no troops to command, and you are a major and outranked by my rank of colonel, you are really in no position to give orders to anyone."

"But I have been sent to take command."

The Green Mountain Boys stack their rifles and laugh.

"Ha, ha, ha. We follow no one but our Colonel Ethan Allen!"

Ethan, quite enjoying the support of his men, smiles.

"I have no time to argue. My boys will not follow you anywhere. I am busy, I have to round up some boats to cross Lake Champlain with the Green Mountain Boys and attack the fort.

I'll tell you what: I will let you march next to me while I attack with my forces, if you stay out of my way. You are very, very lucky that I will even let you come, because out of my force of 200, I only have enough boats for 85. The second and third waves will have to cross later." Benedict Arnold sulks and reluctantly agrees.

The next morning, the Green Mountain Boys are crossing the lake in boats and landing on the New York shore and approaching the fort. Repairs from the former French and Indian War have left one wall caved in, which has been neglected. Only two sentries seem to be guarding the entrance and no one by the damaged wall on the opposite side of the fort.

The Green Mountain Boys climb over the neglected wall undetected and sneak up close to the two guards and the entrance. The sun is just coming up on the morning of May 11, 1775. Ethan Allen whispers his orders:

"I now propose to advance before you, in person, conduct you through the wicket gate, for we must this morning either quit our pretensions to valor or possess ourselves of this fortress in a few minutes. Poise your firelocks and follow me."

Quickly, the Green Mountain Boys follow Ethan Allen and Arnold into the fort and spread out in all directions. The first sentry is totally surprised and drops his musket and runs and hides. The second sentry is attacked by Ethan Allen with profanities, with his sword drawn. After being hit on the head with the blunt side of Ethan's sword, dropped his musket while Ethan Allen yelled in his ear,

"Where be the sleeping quarters of your commandant?"

The frightened sentry replies,

"Up the stairs to your right."

Ethan climbs the stairs with Arnold at his side and approaches the door with his sword raised over his head in a threatening manner. British Lieutenant Feldman was knocking on Captain Delaplace's door in his underwear to warn him of the attack, when he looks at Ethan Allen and Arnold climbing the steps to the captain's quarters.

Ethan Allen says in a booming voice:

"I demand you surrender this fort. Come out of there you goddamned bastard. I demand immediate possession of the fort and all the effects of George the Third."

British Captain Delaplace, now dressed, appears at his open door.

"In whose name?"

"In the name of the great Jehovah and the Continental Congress!" Ethan bellows.

Captain Delaplace, now in shock, sees his men all out on the parade ground being held at gunpoint.

He replies, "We surrender the fort!"

He hands Ethan Allen his sword.

"I shall have my garrison pass in review."

The British flag is lowered and folded and given to Ethan. The garrison passes in review of the victors, led by Ethan Allen in his green-and-yellow uniform. By his side is Benedict Arnold in a red uniform.

"Captains, have your men round up these prisoners and put them in the brig. The officers are to be confined to their quarters. Let your men know that it is almost time to celebrate."

Benedict Arnold is obviously condescending.

"What do you mean by celebrate, Ethan?"

"My men are thirsty and we have discovered the fort's liquor supply. Seth Warner is due to cross the lake about now with the remainder of the Green Mountain Boys and will be arriving momentarily."

"We have successfully captured more than 100 cannons, many mortars, and field pieces, and enough powder and ball to equip the colonials in Boston as we see fit. We have also discovered ninety gallons of rum, for which I now give the order to celebrate. A toast to the Green Mountain Boys! Yea!

The Green Mountain Boys are now chanting:

"Yea! Yea! To Ethan Allen! To our colonel commandant! Yea! Yea!"

The liquor is now flowing as Seth Warner and his company enter the parade grounds and join in on the drunken festivities. Benedict Arnold continues sulking and muttering to himself:

"I cannot believe what I am seeing. Where is the military discipline?"

Arnold was later to write:

"Colonel Allen is a proper man to lead his own people, but entirely unacquainted with military service."

Ethan Allen has taken the fort while the British are asleep, without a single shot being fired, and with no casualties on either side; an amazing act of valor. The weaponry captured will become invaluable to the Colonial war effort.

The Green Mountain Boys find the commandant's liquor supply and celebrate the victory as the remainder of their force under Seth Warner crosses Lake Champlain and joins the drunken festivities in the fort.

Word of Ethan Allen's capture of Fort Ticonderoga reaches the Continental Congress in Philadelphia prior to any official declaration of war with the British. The Congress is frightened and wishes Ethan Allen to return Fort Ticonderoga to the British, for fear that his action might start an all-out war with the British.

Ethan Allen laughs at the stupidity of such a request and prepares to dismantle many cannons in the fort and with teams of oxen, ship cannons to the Minutemen of Massachusetts.

Arnold takes a more accurate inventory of equipment and revises the cannons to more than 200 pieces.

So kids:

"That's the story of one of Ethan Allen's great achievements. He has plenty more and is my favorite hero of the American Revolution."

"Dad, why did Ethan take Benedict Arnold with him?"

"Good question Mike, because Arnold had papers from Connecticut, Ethan had none."

Patty asks:

"Why does Ethan swear so much?

"For effect Patty, People in 1775 were not used to swearing or especially blaspheming so Ethan used it occasionally to separate himself from all mankind as a man afraid of nothing."

"So kids, here is our plan."

"We will sail down the lake and anchor our yacht below the canons at Fort Ticonderoga and take the dingy ashore where you can pretend we are attacking the fort as Ethan did in 1775."

We were up at sunrise while Micheline cooked breakfast aboard. The kids were anxious for the days adventure.

Patty Mike and Micheline at Ft. Ticonderoga, NY

The canon is aimed at our yacht at anchor.

Patty, get ready.

Stand back!

We are up each morning at sunrise and have no TV on board so we are asleep by sundown. The kids look forward to stories at breakfast on board.

Now the kids wanted to know the history of the Battle of Lake Champlain that started with an ambush attack on the mighty British Fleet under the command of Benedict Arnold. We had previously taken the kids to Valcour Island so they were familiar with the site where battle starts.

October 10, 1776 Valcour Island is a large island in Lake Champlain. On the island with the ships anchored offshore, there is a meeting of the captains of the Continental Fleet. Benedict Arnold is addressing his captains.

"Gentlemen, we are about to attack the most powerful navy in the world with our small fleet. The British Navy has the advantage of strength. We have the advantage of surprise. They have no idea there is a naval force on this lake. We also have the advantage of where we choose to attack and how we organize our forces. Here is my plan."

With a model of Valcour Island and models of the ships, he discusses how he plans to hide behind the southern tip of Valcour Island, between the island and the New York shore. Then, with his fleet in an arc formation, which he shows on the model, Benedict Arnold continues: "As the British fleet comes past Valcour Island, we attack and show ourselves in an arc formation and try and draw them to us, one British ship at a time. Some of our bateaux with a cannon in the bow being rowed can do great damage to the early ships that spot us."

"We shall be outnumbered, but if we can keep the British ships in this narrow space, we can do some damage. Remember, our lives to fight another day are more important than the loss of our ships."

October 11, 1776. Sailors of the British Fleet are sailing South on Lake Champlain, totally enjoying the scenery of the Adirondacks and Green Mountains in the distance. The fleet is massive by comparison to Arnold's fleet. Two British sailors on deck are admiring the spectacular scenery.

"Isn't this one of the most beautiful places in the world?"

"It gets even better when we pass Valcour Island, where the lake widens to fourteen miles. You can see further south, where the mountains are even more spectacular on both sides of the lake."

"So beautiful! Is that Valcour Island coming up on our right?"

"Yes, as soon as we pass the southern tip, we enter the wide part of the lake. Look back and see the entire British fleet under sail. Quite a sight, isn't it?"

"Yes it is. Makes you proud to be in His Majesty's service. I see two small boats being rowed up ahead."

With his spyglass, Benedict Arnold sees the approach of the British Fleet, led by a giant three-masted Man of war, the Inflexible, followed by the schooners Maria and Carleton, many small gunboats, and the Thunderer, which is a fourteen-gun floating battery manned by 300. Benedict Arnold issued an order to the captain of the ship Royal Savage.

"Royal Savage, set sail and go meet the enemy with some of our small gunboats. Stay away from the Inflexible, as they might be out of action anyway. I can see they are having trouble going upwind to attack us in this narrow channel."

The battle is underway. Royal Savage heads out and through a mishap tacked to leeward and became easy prey for the many British gunboats. The captain and crew made their escape as the Royal Savage piled on the rocks at Valcour Island. The British schooner Carlton made an attack on the American line of ships and gave the American fleet a few broadsides. Benedict Arnold gave a vocal order which was passed from ship to ship.

"Concentrate all your fire on the Carlton; let's do some damage!"

The American ships concentrate fire and make the British ship so ineffective that the Carlton had to be towed away by rowing craft. That evening, at Valcour Island, on board Arnold's flagship the Congress, a meeting of the captains takes place. The schooner Royal Savage is still burning in the background. Benedict Arnold is addressing his captains.

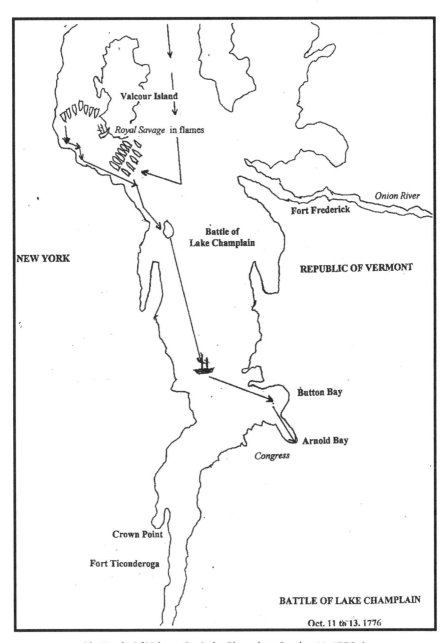

Valcour Island

Royal Savage in flames

Onion River

Fort Frederick

Battle of
Lake Champlain

NEW YORK

REPUBLIC OF VERMONT

Button Bay

Arnold Bay

Congress

Crown Point

Fort Ticonderoga

BATTLE OF LAKE CHAMPLAIN

Oct. 11 th 13. 1776

The Battle Of Valcour On Lake Champlain October 11, 1776. 2.

"Too bad we lost the Philadelphia, which was sunk and the schooner Royal Savage. When the British toppled her rigging, she became a sitting duck. Our Royal Savage captain intelligently beached her to save the men to fight another day. The British have withdrawn, thinking they have won this battle and have us trapped until they finish us off in the morning. Our strategy of forcing the British upwind to attack us worked well. This morning we sure did surprise them, but they are formidable and we will have to retreat to save our men."

An American captain interjects:

"Commander, it sure appears we are trapped. The wind is from the north, so we can't go in that direction. They have closed off on both sides of the island by concentrating most of their downwind."

Arnold replies:

"Captain, they are so busy gloating over their victory that we can wait to pitch dark and leave this narrow passage quietly in single file as close to the New York shore as possible and right under their very noses escape with our entire force. We shall meet at Schuyler Island about ten miles to the south to repair damage to our ships. The Washington has been holed and can be repaired. When they give chase in the morning, we will have a ten-mile head start and leave to the south and engage them when they catch up. If we are hit and damaged to where your crew is endangered, beach your ship to save your crew and head for Crown Point, so we can to evaluate the damage we have done to the British.

"Captain Warner, I want you to lead this single line of ships in the Trumbull. I will take up the rear as the last ship in the Congress."

Another captain asks,

"How much damage to the British today?"

"We sank several British gunboats, and when their frigate Carlton went off course to the center of our arc, we did a lot of damage to that ship. The British got lucky when two more gunboats were able to tow the Carlton away. If we were not here today, the British would already be attacking Fort Ticonderoga. You are all fulfilling a valuable service to your country. If we could just hold them off until the ice comes and the lake is frozen solid, we will have delayed their attack until next year. If we just hold them off until ice, we will be victorious."

THAT NIGHT, IN DARKNESS ON LAKE CHAMPLAIN A single ship glides by close to the New York shoreline quietly, a smaller ship follows, and you can barely hear the oars slapping the water. Then another large ship and still more smaller ones until all is very quiet as they have all escaped.

FLAMING COLORS AT ARNOLD BAY The next day, the British fleet is surrounded by morning fog. British Captain Pringle alarms General Carlton.

"General, General. The Americans are gone!"

"What? Damn! We had them trapped. How did they do that? How did they escape?

Sound the alarm to the rest of the fleet and signal them to give chase as soon as the fog lifts and the wind comes up."

LAKE CHAMPLAIN. 2 PM, on a Friday, the thirteenth.

The American fleet is at Schuyler Island. Repairs are not fully completed yet but the ships are seaworthy. The wind is just starting to come up, blowing southward, when Commander Arnold gives the command:

"Set sail...anchors away."

The American fleet is underway with the British fleet ten miles behind, having also started at the same time when the wind came up. The British fleet is closing in on the slower boats. Benedict Arnold is directing a captain at the helm.

"They are closing on us. Raise all the sail we have, and put up the lateen sails as well."

The Captain appears worried.

"Commander, with all that sail, we are leaving our own ship, Washington, in the distance."

"I know. If the British man of war Inflexible catches the Washington out here in the middle of the lake, she will strike her colors. She is too far from shore to beach the ship and save the crew."

"Commander, they are faster ships. What will happen to us?"

"We are trying to make a run for Crown Point, just north of Ticonderoga, where we have shore batteries to help us. Judging from our speed today, I do not think we can make it. The British have more sail area to fill with wind, and longer water line length to displace their giant size. Most of our smaller vessels will beach themselves as I have instructed their captains."

"We still have the advantage of picking the place to do battle with them, and judging from the rate they are catching up with us, and the direction of the wind, I will aim to a tiny bay inside Button Bay on the Grants (Vermont) side of the lake."

"But Commander, we are supposed to meet at Crown Point on the New York side."

"Crown Point, New York, yes, but the wind direction determines where we do battle, and if we end up on the Grants side of the lake, so be it. Our job is to hurt or deter the British Navy. The mission comes first."

"Commander, three of their biggest ships are closing in!" "Head for Button Bay in the Grants. When they get alongside, let 'em have it, so we can hold 'em while some of our smaller boats can get away!"

A battle ensues on the broad lake with three of His Majesty's ships against the Congress. Cannons roar as the Congress does some damage to all three British ships, but they keep pursuing the Americans all the way to Button Bay on the Grants side of Lake Champlain.

"Enter Button Bay off Vergennes and head for the tiny narrow bay within Button Bay in the southern part of Button Bay."

"I see puffs of smoke from the entire British Fleet. We are getting showered with shot. I can even smell their gunpowder now that they are getting so close to us. Commander, what are we going to do?"

"I am going to beach the Congress in that tiny bay where the big British ships cannot maneuver. Remove the cannons, ball and ammunition, and crew and torch the ship."

The three British frigates chase Arnold in Button Bay and heave to and hold back as they observe the even smaller bay off Button Bay that Arnold has sailed into. The British deep draft ships await in the larger Button Bay to see Arnold become trapped approaching a dead end.

Arnold gives the fateful order:

"Beach the ship here. Every man ashore with all cannons, balls, powder, and muskets before we torch her. We are only about twelve miles from Crown Point. We march from here and cross by ferry."

Three big ships of the British fleet trap the Congress in this tiny, dead-end bay inside Button Bay. General Carlton points out to his captain.

"We have them now. We will wait until they try and come out of this tiny bay where we have them trapped." "Look, General, they have set their own ship afire."

General Carlton stares in admiration.

"A great strategy. I stand in awe at the courage of the Americans. Arnold refuses to strike his colors and surrender. I will bet they took all the weaponry off the ship before they set it afire. Look at the American colors now in flames. I am sure they are on their way to Crown Point, where they will try to ambush us by both land batteries and the remaining ships that we didn't capture. Who knows how many more ships they have waiting for us?"

"What now, General?"

General Carlton is now visibly disappointed. "We never expected opposition by an American navy. It is time to regroup and repair our ships. Head north to the Richelieu River and return to Montreal."

DAYS LATER AT THE CROWN POINT REDOUBT

Benedict Arnold is addressing the survivors of the Battle of Lake Champlain. "Officers and men of the first American naval battle, the following are the results of the Battle of Lake Champlain and the Battle of Valcour.[2]

"Out of fifteen American ships, only four returned to Crown Point, the Trumble, the Enterprise, the Savage, and the New York. Eleven ships were lost, ten in the Battle of Valcour and one in the battle on Lake Champlain on the broad part of the lake. Over eighty Americans were killed or wounded, twenty-seven of which were from my ship, the Congress. One hundred and ten men were captured, and all the rest escaped and returned to Crown Point. The British will claim this as a major victory.

Yet we know the truth: They are back in Montreal with their tail between their legs, and the ice will freeze Lake Champlain, and we will not see these cowards again until next year. So...What navy drove back the British?" A sailor in the crowd responds: "The United States Navy!"

From Partridge Cove, we sail to the Vermont side of Lake Champlain for dinner at Basin Harbor Club, Vergennes. After eating on board each night, it is nice to have a formal dinner in a fancy place.

---

2   Roach Jr., John P., *The Fourteenth State*. 2007. Authorhouse, Bloomington, IN.

Arnold Bay is so similar to Partridge Bay as a small place to beach the Congress.

Patty stays aboard while Mike goes fishing in Partridge Cove, Lake Champlain

chapter xxxv
JIMMY SETS UP THE BOAT SHOW

MY BROTHER Jim saw how rattled I get setting up the Montreal Boat Show each year with cranes lifting up each yacht and placing it in position next to scaffolding that people climb up to view the yachts. I always envisioned them dropping a yacht.

Jimmy offered:

"You relax, your nerves are shot, I'll take care of the set-up this year.

"Really"?

"Sure, I can do it. Just show up when the show opens and everything will be ready. Go get a sun tan so you look like a sailor.

"Wow! What a brother."

Behind Jeep is new, two bedroom, beachfront cabin on stilts at Long Bay Resort, Tortola.

So off I went to Tortola again, this time with Micheline and my parents. A first time for both. Long Bay Hotel has just opened a few cabins on stilts over the breaking waves, that my mother would love, so it is a perfect time to treat my parents to ten days in Tortola.

Took my Dad in Jeep to Tortola's Highest Point, Long Bay Beach below.

Everyone had a good time, my parents loved my favorite place in the sun. Long Bay Resort. We spent one day at Caneel Bay Plantation on St. John as well.

When the vacation was over, I had a sailor tan, for the boat show and I arrived at the opening and there is my brother Jimmy smiling with everything in place.

"I told you I could do it."

"You sure did Jimmy, great job! I owe you big time"

"Forget it, John, I'll be glad to do it again next year

Bay Harbor Yachts, Ltd. Largest Yacht Display at Montreal Boat Show.

chapter xxxvi
FLORIDA & DISNEYWORLD

MICHELINE AND I took the kids for a week in Clearwater, Florida where we stayed on a 30 foot S2 Aft cabin Yacht at Clearwater Marina.

With a home base at Clearwater Beach, Disneyworld was their number one place to visit. A parent is so rewarded just seeing the excitement of his children at each Disneyworld experience.

Mike at Disneyworld

Patty racing Mike at Disneyworld

With a whole week at Clearwater Beach there were many other Florida activities like taking the yacht out into the Gulf Of Mexico for a full days sail. Cooking with the kids aboard and even experiencing Florida Deep Sea Fishing.

Mike and Patty at Clearwater Beach Marina, Florida

Skateboarding at Clearwater Beach, Florida

chapter xxxvii

MONTREAL

EACH YEAR I would spend two weeks in Montreal, Canada setting up for the Boat Show at the Place Bonaventure. I eventually became the largest and most prominent displayer of yachts with 13 yachts on display at the same time, some as large as 36 feet.

Yacht arriving at Bay Harbor Yachts

Micheline being fluent in French was a great help during these years. I was attempting to stay at IBM until my 15th anniversary to retire but my sideline business was growing too fast. I resigned from IBM at 14 ½ years of service and became a millionaire within a year.

With profits from Bay Harbor Yachts, Ltd. I purchased land with 2400 feet of deep water protected lake frontage to start development of a marina in North Hero, Vermont only 45 minutes from downtown Montreal.

After attending a week long course in marina development in Boston, MA sponsored by dock manufacturers, I felt confident in entering this new venture.

I also purchased a secluded lakefront home called Five Oaks in North Hero, Vermont on an opposite shore from the proposed marina. By water Five Oaks was a mile from the marina, by land it was 6 miles by car. We could observe the action at the marina in total privacy across the bay.

Vacationing with Micheline on the beach at Nisbet Plantation, Nevis.

Five Oaks was 35 Miles north of Malletts Bay where my first Bay Harbor Yachts office was prospering in the Burlington, VT marketplace of 40,000 population.

Once moved in to Five Oaks I started construction of Marina International across Pelots Bay from our home and only 45 miles from downtown Montreal an even larger marketplace of two million population.

Lakefront home with lake on three sides, Five Oaks, Savage Point, North Hero, VT

The Five Oaks were quite large.

235-Boat Marina In N. Hero Awaits Permit Approval

By ELOISE HEDBOR
Free Press Correspondent

ARTIST'S RENDERING OF NORTH HERO'S MARINA INTERNATIONALE
... marina would provide seasonal work for 25

NORTH HERO — A multimillion-dollar marina with facilities to dock up to 235 boats, as well as a pump-out station, a restaurant and assorted boat services, is being developed on the west shore of North Hero.

John Roach Jr., president of Bay Harbour Yachts Ltd., which is developing Marina Internationale, said Wednesday the onshore boat sales and the travel lift on Pelots Point have been in operation since last fall.

Permit applications for the additional facilities have been made, he said. Once these permits, including development approval under Act 250, are granted, there will be an additional $1.5 million investment, he said.

Roach said he expects to have about 25 seasonal job openings, excluding the restaurant, and will attempt to hire locally.

Bay Harbour Yachts moved its headquarters to Marina Internationale last fall, Roach said, but will continue its sales operation in Mallets Bay, Colchester. The company had nearly $1 million in boat sales, primarily sailboats, last year, and Roach said he expects sales well over $1 million this year.

The marina was planned, Roach said, because "There comes a time in boat sales where you have sold so many boats and made so many friends among the people you have sold boats to that you want to do something more than just sell them a boat and wave goodbye."

But Marina Internationale goes beyond that, he said. It is envisioned as "a full marina resort complex capable of serving the yachtsman, the town and the state of Vermont."

The marina is on 13 acres on Pelots Point with 2,350 feet of deep-water frontage. Roach said he doesn't expect dredging will be required even for large sailboats. The bay is well-protected from wind by its natural formation and the Rutland Railroad fill.

Roach suggested that even Samuel de Champlain, when he passed this spot in 1609, might have admired its safe harbor.

In addition to the 235 slips, each with power and water, plans include a grocery store and ship's chandlery called Boutique Nautique. Farther in the future is a restaurant on the tip of the point.

The pump-out facility, once it is approved by the state, will be on the only one north of Burlington on the broad lake. There are such facilities in Mallets Bay and on Burton Island in the Great East Bay, neither on the main lake.

Late last year Bay Harbour Yachts received both North Hero and Act 250 permits for launching, hauling and winter storage at the site.

Problems of waste disposal and road maintenance have to be resolved before permits are granted for the docks and other facilities. But, Roach said, "good progress" is being made in those areas.

Roach said he expects the new marina, closer to Canada than any similar facility on Lake Champlain, will "serve as a melting pot of fresh ideas between people of different cultures, backgrounds and interests."

Burlington Free Press

Design of proposed Marina Internationale, North Hero, VT

Marina Internationale opens in North Hero, Vermont.

chapter xxxviii
A TRAGIC YEAR 1980

EVERYTHING APPEARS to be going right, we sold more yachts at the Montreal Boat Show than ever before. All summer long my brother Jim was rigging yachts for new customers and taking some customers out for a sail as well.

Each September I would travel to Holland, Michigan to the S2 Yacht Factory for a weekend at Point West Resort on the shores of Lake Michigan. This time I offered to take my brother Jimmy and my son Michael for all the help they were to my yacht sales business.

Micheline, Michael, Jimmy and I were met at the Airport by a limo and taken to Point West Resort. Jimmy and Michael quickly got into their bathing suits for swim in Lake Michigan. Jimmy said:

"I will stay close to shore to watch Michael and wait until you get there."

Jimmy saw us coming to join them and said he was going leave Michael now, so we sat on the beach. A few minutes later Jimmy yelled out help! I quickly went in the lake after him and swam up to him and said:

"What's the matter, do you have cramps"?

"No, neither of us are getting out of here because of the tide."

"Well try putting your face in the water and swim hard, kicking your feet like this.

I got maybe 20 feet toward shore and saw the futility of my efforts and yelled to Micheline on shore.

"Micheline, get help! This is serious."

Micheline ran up and down the beach getting help. Meanwhile the waves were huge and pulling me back out away from shore.

I was already frightened and getting hypothermia and realized I could not take much more of this. I was pounded by about ten waves, to the point that I said aloud:

"Guardian Angel where are you! I can only take one more wave"

I took the wave and came up for air, and saw before a man sitting in the middle of a rubber truck tube, who yelled to me,

"Grab hold."

He towed me ashore, then went out for my brother who was no longer to be found. My son saw his Dad cry and he cried too, for his Uncle Jim.

Next, I called my parents who were devastated by the tragic loss of their youngest son.

They did not find his body for a week. I learned later that we were both caught in a rip tide and all we had to do was swim parallel to the shore away from wall causing the danger.

Later that year Micheline and I took the kids trout fishing is a small lake north of Lac St. Jean, in Quebec, Canada. When we returned home I received a telephone call from my second wife informing me that she was diagnosed with cancer of the pancreas.

A month later she had to return to Tijuana, Mexico for more treatments and I asked Micheline if she would go with her, because I did not want her traveling alone. Micheline had never been to California or Mexico, so she was happy to go with her, which she did.

When Micheline returned, I was told that her cancer is hopeless and my spiritual second wife would be dead before year end.

I also filed for a divorce from my third wife Micheline by year end.

What a tragic year was 1980. The death of my brother Jimmy followed by my divorcing my third wife followed by the death of my second wife.

Fortunately however, my children were there for me when I needed them most.

My son Michael learned to drive the Bay Harbor Yachts pick up truck on the Marina property. Any time there was a chance to move something, Mike jumped in the cab and drove the truck.

North Hero had a population of only 400 so any time errands needed to be done, Mike gladly took the Bay Harbor Yachts truck to get more driving experience. With the tragic loss of my brother Jimmy, Mike was there to help when he could.

The last picture of Jimmy with Michael on the day of the fateful swim.

Patty, a champion at Colchester High School

chapter xxxix

OCCUPATION CHANGE

THE BEAUTIFUL Pat Penoyer becomes my fourth wife. As I no longer need documents, ceremony, and all that stuff that weddings are all about as we just love each other and she moves into Five Oaks with me.

Pat is 25 years younger than I and graduated Summa Cum Laude in Accounting from Chaplain College. Pat's skill as an accountant came in handy as the yacht business was taking a downturn as interest rates were climbing.

Pat and I did the Montreal Boat Show together and stayed at the Chateau Champlain across from the Boat Show and could see that business is bad. Reganomics had by this time raised interest rates to 22% and no one was considering the purchase of a yacht. So we just had a good time doing Montreal restaurants for 10 days hoping interest rates would return to normal by summer.

Pat Penoyer

I have had so many good times, that it is time for me to experience the bad times. The handwriting is on the wall. Without yacht sales my business will eventually go bankrupt. One of the sailors, Henry J. Maloney, that bought a yacht from me saw my predicament and offered me a job at MONY, Mutual Life Insurance Co. of New York, claiming I am the best salesman he ever saw, because he didn't even want a yacht when he bought one from me.

My daughter Patty called to ask if I would take her to New York City for a job interview in New York City for physical fitness specialty as a trainer.

Patty and I flew to New York for her interview and she was offered the job. The interviewer did alert Patty to the idea of culture shock that could happen to her coming from rural Vermont. After the interview I took Patty to the top of the Empire State Building to look over the city where she was considering to relocate.

After careful thought for a few days, Patty elected to stay in Vermont.

During November and December I studied for my Insurance License and nervously took the exam. I was never good at tests so this was crunch time and I was frightened. When the results came in, my manager, Henry Maloney told me that I got the highest mark ever recorded in the State of Vermont. I was happy and Pat Penoyer was proud of me. I was pumped and ready to go to work in an entirely new occupation.

In my first year with MONY I qualified for the prestigious Million Dollar Round Table and did so again in my second year to get my MDRT Plaque, that I proudly displayed in my office.

Out of curiosity, I asked Henry, my manager:

"What was my mark on the insurance exam two years ago, you never did tell me?"

"P", He said."

"I thought you said I got the highest mark ever recorded in the state of Vermont."

"You did, P is the highest mark, because it is either P or an F. I told you the truth."

"Ha, and all the time I believed you. You are very funny."

MONY was a good company to start with in the insurance business. I won a sales contest for a free trip to Vancouver, Canada. Pat and I really enjoyed the Tea House in Stanley Park, the Steam Clock and all the totem poles and the various Vancouver sites. MONY also provided me with

Patty graduates from University of Vermont with a Bachelor of Science Degree.

advanced training in financial planning at University of Southern California and Notre Dame University as well as University of Houston.

During this time I helped my son Mike get his first apartment in downtown Burlington and Patty graduated from the University of Vermont with a Bachelor of Science Degree.

My first wife Jackie graciously invites all New Jersey relatives to her home after the graduation ceremony where both the Frenette and Roach families honor Patty.

Mike and his friend moved to Daytona Beach Florida where Mike got a job with Treasure Island Inn. The two boys, stopped to see Mike's Grandparents in New Jersey on the way to Florida. My Dad called me to let me know how touched he was that Mike visited all grown up.

Michael and Patty Roach

Patty Roach Davis

chapter xxxiv
PATTY ROACH DAVIS

GAVE AWAY my daughter Patty to Sam Charles Davis in a beautiful wedding in 1987 at Calis Vermont. Patty and Sam moved to New Hampshire and eventually to Boston. Pat and I visited the newleyweds at both locations and they seem to be the most happy couple. We took them to dinner at Henry David, in NH and drank a lot of beer and when in Boston took them to lunch at Harvard Square in Cambridge, MA

Isn't Patty beautiful?

chapter xxxv
CARRABEAN CRUISE

Pat my 4ᵗʰ wife (common law), at Moro Castle, Puerto Rico.

THIS CRUISE visited Martinique, Dominica, St. Vincent, Bequia, St. Kitts and St. Thomas. I had been to St. Thomas often before and knew the Bomba Charger could take us to Tortola for Pat's first visit. Pat got a chance to see my favorite Long Bay Resort, Tortola.

Pat at Long Bay Resort, Tortola, BVI

Pat Penoyer at Marina Internationale

chapter xxxvi
FINANCIAL DYNAMICS CORPORATION

MAKING THE Million Dollar Round Table two years in a row, I decided to start my own business once again, first by becoming a General Agent with Transamerica and hiring my own agents and then by Incorporating my new company, Financial Dynamics Corporation.

I traveled to each town and hamlet in the state of Vermont and hired 120 agents and brokers that could put their business through Financial Dynamics Corporation and so many did so, making my new company a successful operation.

With money coming in, I gave a lot back with sales contests for the largest producers, with trips to Chateau Frontenac in Canada, Sagamore Hotel on Lake George, NY, Chateau Laurier in Ottawa, Canada and Chatham Bars Inn on Cape Cod, MA and Harborside Inn at Martha's Vineyard, MA. I took Patty and her husband Sam on the two Massachusetts weekends as well.

Financial Dynamics Corporation

Pat Penoyer in my Burlington, Vermont office.

My office and Conference Room at rear overlooking Burlington Airport.

Pat Penoyer and I on a Caribbean Cruise

Pat visiting FDC West Coast Office, La Jolla, CA

Mom, Dad and Pat Penoyer at Point Pleasant on the Jersey Shore

Pat Penoyer at the Tea House in Stanley Park, Vancouver, BC, Canada.

chapter xxxvii
THE BACHELOR YEAR

FOR REALLY no other reason than it was time for both us to move on, Pat Penoyer and I amicably separated. She remains one of my best friends to this day. I moved to a lakefront condo in Burlington, VT. The Ethan Allen Club was redecorating and they pretty much furnished my place with exquisite used furniture at bargain prices.

My company Financial Dynamics Corporation was growing and I opened up a West Coast Office in La Jolla, California; a place that I had selected years before as the ideal place to retire.

I visited my son Michael in Daytona Beach Florida where he showed me around Daytona. He took me to my first Jai Lai and first Dog Track, both are Florida type activities and I enjoyed them both. Mike enjoys being a kid and now living in a beach town for which he gets due credit, for getting to the warm weather even before his Dad.

I have never been a bachelor, it seems I have been married all my life. This was a new experience for me. The first few weeks I went out a lot and came to see that I was becoming a bar fly, meeting no one of consequence. I came to the conclusion that I would rather stay home and listen to classical music on my stereo and just go out on Saturday nights.

On a second visit to see my son in Daytona Beach Florida he took me to *Epcot Center*, the new theme park that just opened. Over a few beers, I let Mike know that I was getting tired of the Vermont winters. I purchased a Time Share on a cliff overlooking the Pacific Ocean, in Del Mar, California, just north of La Jolla.

I let Mike know that I plan to permanently move to California as the

Vermont winters are too severe the older you become. Mike understood and laughed.

Mike told me that he recently changed jobs and was now working for Taco Bell. I mentioned that there are plenty of Taco Bell's in California, in fact there is one in La Jolla.

"How would you like to investigate a transfer to the La Jolla, Taco Bell? You could be near your Dad when he settles down in La Jolla."

"Sounds like a good idea, I've never been to California."

"How about, I buy you airline tickets from Daytona to San Francisco, CA. and once there, I can meet you with a car rental and we can drive down the entire coast. You can see Monterey, Big Sur, Malibu, Los Angeles and Santa Monica as we drive down the coast to La Jolla where I can arrange an interview for you."

'Sure, I'll take my vacation."

"Good. I will return to Burlington and send you airline tickets to San Francisco and be waiting there at the gate when you get off the plane. We will stay at *Wave Crest*, my Time Share in Del Mar for as long as you like to get used to the area."

chapter xxxviii
CALIFORNIA DREAMING

I MET Mike at the San Francisco Airport and rented a Lincoln Continental for our trip down the coast. After seeing the sights of San Francisco we headed for the coast at Monterey stopped in at *Sly McFly's* for a few beers and walked about the town that John Steinbeck wrote so much about.

Our next stop was Carmel the small tourist town that Michael enjoyed so much, followed by driving through the Big Sur with such outstanding scenery. Before you knew it we were in Santa Barbara and visited the Mission and enjoyed the city. The next stops were Malibu Beach and Santa Monica where I showed Mike my favorite British Pub. *Ye Old King's Inn* where they still play darts amid an atmosphere serving the best Fish & Chips around.

"So what do you think of California so far Mike?"

"Seems like the further south we go the better it gets."

In Los Angeles I took Mike to *Universal Studios* and *La Brea Tar Pits* before dinner atop the *Transamerica Tower* with views of the entire city.

South of Los Angeles we hit all the beach towns on the way to San Diego and we are still ahead of schedule so we went all the way to Tijuana, Mexico, for some Mexican food on Avenue Revolution, and a Caesar Salad where it was invented.

From Tijuana we returned to my time share in Del Mar, CA to prepare for Michael's Taco Bell interview.

Needless to say, Mike got the job and his boss Terry, said to me,

"They just don't have kids like that around here. If I asked him to clean the rest rooms with a toothbrush he would gladly do it," he said laughing. "Thanks for bringing Mike for me to meet him."

"Ok Dad I got the job, as Assistant Manager of La Jolla Taco Bell as soon as possible. What do we do now?"

"Let's find you a place to live in the village of La Jolla."

We looked at a few places that were looking for room mates and Mike found a nice place within walking distance of Taco Bell and put a deposit on it, leaving only the question of how to move to California.

"Can you fit all your worldly possessions in that tiny car of yours" I asked.

"Yes, I could."

"And me too?"

"Why you?"

"Because we could drive across the country together and see the many National Parks on the way."

"The whole country? What a great idea. I'm ready, let's do it."

"You pick the day and drive from Daytona to Jacksonville and I will meet you at the Airport and we will start our cross country trip from there.'

"Great it will take me a day to drive from Daytona to Jacksonville. I'll stay overnight and meet your plane in the morning."

So there was our plan for another adventure with a new job awaiting Michael and all the California Dreaming about to become reality.

chapter xl
FATHER & SON CROSS COUNTRY TRIP

MET MICHAEL in Jacksonville, Florida and admired how well he packed all his worldly possessions into what we call *the Blue Minnow* the tiniest of Pontiacs.

As I got in the passenger seat, Mike said, "Let's go!"

We head west on Interstate 10 traversing the panhandle of Florida, then crossing Alabama and Mississippi on our way to our first destination Bourbon Street, New Orleans, Louisiana.

Mike and I had a great time in New Orleans and stayed the night, planning to be in San Antonio, Texas the next day.

Bourbon Street, New Orleans, LA

Jazz Band, New Orleans.

We stayed in San Antonio Texas the second night preparing to get an early start in the morning alternating between we two drivers.

On the road again, the next morning with Mike driving, The endless straight empty roads, a police car started his siren behind Mike, so Mike pulled to the side of the road.

Mike rolled down the window and the policeman said:

"Boy, your going 100 miles and hour. You could hit a deer."

"Yes sir."

"Does your Daddy know you drive that fast?"

"I don't know, that's him sitting next to me. Ask him."

Needless to say, Mike got his ticket and before the day was done, I got one too.

By the end of the day we were tired and pulled into a motel in El Paso, Texas before looking for a place for dinner.

"Where we going to eat," asked Mike.

"How about Juarez Mexico, right across the border."

"Yeah, I could go for some Mexican food and maybe a Carona or two."

The Alamo, San Antonio, Texas

Dinner at Tower of the America's, San Antonio, Texas

River-walk, San Antonio, Texas

The Blue Minnow at Guadalupe Mountains National Park, Texas

Local Bar, Juarez, Mexico.

Two Corona's?
Returning from Juarez, Mexico to El Paso, Texas.

The Blue Minnow entering Carlsbad Caverns National Park

Inside Carlsbad Caverns National Park

The next morning on day four we are finally out of Texas crossing the New Mexico Border heading to Carlsbad Caverns National Park.

"Hey Mike, it is only day four and we are already in Tucson. We could be in La Jolla, CA tomorrow as we are way ahead of schedule with the two of us driving across the United States. Have you seen enough National Parks yet?"

"No, let's see some more."

"What do you say that we stop heading west and head north to the Grand Canyon and Utah visiting more parks on the way.

"Yes! Let's do it."

Montezuma National Monument contains a Native American Pueblo built in the side of a cliff that we found interesting.

Continuing north we gain altitude and arrive at the snow covered Grand Canyon National Park.

Saguaro National Park, Tucson, Arizona

Montezuma National Monument

Grand Canyon National Park, Arizona
Could you back up a little bit and smile? Ha!

Grand Canyon National Park, Arizona

Blue Minnow makes it to Zion National Park, Utah

Golden Nugget Casino, Las Vegas, Nevada

Hoover Dam, Nevada

Mike at his home in La Jolla, California

So our trip is complete, Mike is home in La Jolla, California. I took Mike and his manager Terry to dinner at Jake's in Del Mar. The waiter poured water in everyone's glass and when Terry was about to drink, Mike said:

"Doesn't California water come from the Colorado River"?

"Yes, he said."

"What is the name of the river at the bottom of the Grand Canyon?"

"The Colorado River."

"Why"?

"I wouldn't drink that water if I were you."

"Why?'

"We did what little boy's do at the edge of a steep canyon. Ha!"

Everyone laughed and it set the tone for the dinner to celebrate Mike's new adventure as Assistant Manager of the La Jolla, CA Taco Bell.

Mike drove me to the airport for my flight back to Burlington, VT and leaving was difficult for both of us, so I gave Mike a hug and said I will move to La Jolla as soon as I can.

chapter xli
WHAT ABOUT PATTY?

MIKE HAD his cross-country adventure now it's Patty's turn, after all I have two kids, so I invited Patty and Sam to my time share in Del Mar, California. Patty was excited and said Sam can't get the time off but she would love to visit, so I sent her plane tickets.

Patty stayed with me for a week at Wave Crest, my ocean front time share in Del Mar.

Oceanfront 2 BR, 2 Bath, time share at Wave Crest, Del Mar, California

Patty at Wave Crest, Del Mar, CA

Patty at Hotel del Coronado, Coronado, CA

La Jolla Cove

La Jolla Cliff Walk.

183

Old Town, San Diego, CA

SAN DIEGO CHAMBER ORCHESTRA

Donald Barra, Conductor
The Empire Brass Quintet

March 13, 1989
March 14, 1989

There have been some changes in this evening's program. The program will be performed as follows:

HANDEL	The Water Music, Suite
GABRIELI	Canzone e Sonate
PURCELL	The Fairy Queen, Suite
HANDEL	The Royal Fireworks

Intermission

DIAMOND	Rounds for String Orchestra
COPLAND	Simple Gifts
RAVEL	Habanera
DEBUSSY	Suite Bergamasque
BERNSTEIN	Mass, selections

Took Patty to La Jolla, Chamber Orchestra.

Mike and Patty at Wave Crest

Pat and Dad at Mike's Home, La Jolla, CA

Pat and her Dad in Tijuana, Mexico

Pat and Mike know how to relax.

Patty at Wave Crest Pool.

Cocktail Time at Wave Crest

chapter xlii
SOUTHERN CARIBBEAN CRUISE

EMBARKED ON Chandris Cruise Line's (now Celebrity) SS, Amaricanis at San Juan Puerto Rico bound for the Southern Caribbean, visiting ports in Barbados, St. Maarten, St. Thomas, Guadeloupe, St. Lucia and Martinique.

Cruising as a bachelor is something I am not used to. But off I go for the pure adventure of it. I met a really nice gal, Maggi Stacy on this cruise. She was married and traveling with her sister but was so much fun to be around that she made this cruise very enjoyable.

Maggi at Le Toc Resort, St. Lucia, that overlooks our ship SS Americanis.

Maggi with her sister Jean Waters on beach in Guadeloupe.

Maggi and Jean ordering dinner.

Maggi at the Fort, St Lucia

Maggi

chapter xliii
BURLINGTON VERMONT

RETURNING TO Burlington after the cruise in time for Patty's Birthday.

Patty and Sam at my lakefront condo, Burlington, VT.

Marlene Pollock visits from Montreal.

Patty and Sam (right center), join us for Martha's Vineyard FDC Awards Weekend.

194

Fathers Day with my daughter at Vermont condo.

Patty and her Dad at Stowe VT, Mozart Festival.

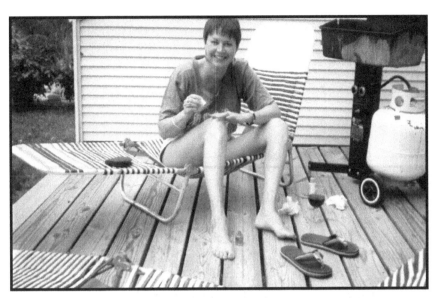

Marlene visits my condo again.

Picnic at Mozart Festival with Marlene, Shelburne, VT

My Birthday 1989

Marlene takes me out for my birthday with the most remarkable home made birthday card that really touched me. Her card follows:

Collage cover from Marlene's home made Birthday Card

JOHN'S FAVOURITE THINGS

Lyrics by OSCAR HAMMERSTEIN II / Music by RICHARD RODGERS   THE SOUND OF MUSIC (1959)

Homemade Birthday Card from Marlene.

Pat Saldi FDC Agent of the Year at Sagamore Resort, Lake George, NY

Pat Saldi and husband at high tea, Sagamore Resort, Lake George, NY

Patty and Sam eventually returned to Vermont where Patty bought a Morgan Horse and did a lot of riding.

They would visit me in Burlington where I took them to their first Opera, La Boheme, that was also my first opera that I finally enjoyed after my mistake of avoiding opera for 20 years, just because the first one was a bummer and sung in English. We all have been to many operas since, so operas finally join ballet and symphony as wonderfully entertaining cultural events.

I became so involved in Opera that I became a patron of the Arts for San Diego Opera and was so moved by the idealism of Richard Wagner's Flying Dutchman that I wrote a book on Wagner's Operas.[3]

With Patty and Sam back in the Burlington area, I was able to take them to Rimsky-Korsakov's *Scheherazade* Ballet, at Place des Arts, in Montreal. Choreography by Diaghilev whom Rimsky-Korsakov could not refuse. This ballet was so good that I later wrote a book about Rimsky-Korsakov. [4]

---

3   Roach, John P. Jr. Triumph of the Swan, A Biographical Novel of Composer Richard Wagner and King Ludwig II of Bavaria. 2009. Author House, Bloomington, IN

4   Roach, John P. Jr. The Mighty Kuchka, A Biographical Novel of Nikolai Rimsky-Korsakov *and the Russian Five*. 2009. Author House, Bloomington, IN.

Mike visits from La Jolla, CA

Took Marie, from Burlington, VT and Mike for a day in Ensenada, Mexico

Lyn Leah using my Office at Financial Dynamics Corporation, Burlington, VT.

Financial Dynamics Corporation, Burlington. VT, office.

Financial Dynamics Corporatio
INVESTMENTS—PORTFOLIO MANAGEMENT— FINANCIAL PLANNING
Burlington Vermont—La Jolla California

Financial Dynamics Corporation, La Jolla, CA office.

It did not take Mike long to be promoted to Manager of the La Jolla Taco Bell where he really enjoyed his job.

Visiting Mike so often in La Jolla, CA he bought tickets for me to see my first Charger game, where the San Diego Chargers lost to the New York Jets. He further took me for my first visit to the top of Mt. Soledad in La Jolla to see the spectacular view. In both cases Mike was a major influence on his Dad. Years later in 2007 my book *Mt. Soledad Love Story* was published. [5] Season tickets to the Chargers were purchased and we have attended so many games that I am still a fan.

---

5   Roach, John P. Jr., *Mt. Soledad Love Story*, 2007. Author House, Bloomington IN.

Deborah J. Johnson

chapter xliv
DULCINEA

THE FEW women I dated during this bachelor year helped me through a very lonely year and each deserves my thanks for putting up with me.

Well my quest is over, I have found my Dulcinea, the ideal woman for me, the delightful Deborah Johnson whom I met on October 18, 1989.

Debbie and I lived together in Burlington, VT from October 1989 to August, 1990 when I moved to La Jolla, CA to join my son as promised, with Debbie joining me for life the day after Christmas 1990.[6]

---

6   Roach, John P. Jr., *Thanks for the Memories*, 2011. *An Open Kitchen Cookbook and Travelogue.* Author House, Bloomington, IN

THE LOVE STORY CONTINUES.

The romantic and exciting twenty-one year love story of
Deborah and John continues in the following two books:

AROUND THE WORLD IN A WHEELCHAIR.

Thanks for the Memories: An Open Kitchen Cookbook & Travelogue

www.JPRoach.org

Also available from Amazon, Barnes & Noble,
Author House and most on-line retailers

travelogue

1936
HERE'S JOHNNY!

Jersey City, NJ   Born to Alberta and John Roach at Christ
                          Hospital.

Jersey City, NJ   First spanking at delivery by Doctor,
                          made me cry.

1937
SUMMER VACATION

Union City, NJ   Mom and Dad had apartment in Union
                          City. Saw city from stroller.

Leonardo, NJ   Grandparents summer cottage. Gentle
                          waves at Sandy Hook Bay.

1938
MOM AND DAD'S NEW HOME

FAIR LAWN, NJ — Visited new home construction each week. Played in dirt pile.

FAIL LAWN, NJ — Watched construction of new home.

1939
RAN AWAY FROM HOME

FAIR LAWN, NJ — With peanut butter & Jelly sandwich left home.

1940
BECAME A FREE THINKER AT AGE FIVE

ROCHELLE PARK, NJ — Nuns embarrassed to pick me up at Public School Kindergarten.

FAIRLAWN, NJ — Caught hell at school, caught hell at home, Johnny is a bad boy!

1941
FIRST GRADE

ROCHELLE PARK, NJ — Chosen to crown the Virgin Mary in May Procession.

ROCHELLE PARK, NJ — Bantam weight boxing match at Sacred Heart School.

211

1942
PARENTS BUY LARGER HOME IN GLEN ROCK, NJ

LEONARDO, NJ

Spent time at Grandparents bungalow for Summer vacation.

FAIR LAW, NJ

Dad made me a workbench so I could learn woodworking.

HUDSON RIVER CRUISE

Grandpa took me from NYC to Sandy Hook, NJ on Hudson River Cruise

GLEN ROCK, NJ

Family moves to older home in Glen Rock, NJ

GLEN ROCK, NJ

Enter Second Grade at Richard E. Byrd, Public School.

ELLIS ISLAND, NJ

Mom took me to the Statue of Liberty, we climbed up to the crown.

1943
FIRST PUPPY

GLEN ROCK, NJ

Named the puppy Spot, like Dick & Jane and Spot. Not too bright.

GLEN ROCK, NJ

Mom and Dad plant Victory Garden during World War II.

GLEN ROCK, NJ

Dad builds 60 foot walk through grape arbor to hide Victory Garden.

GLEN ROCK, NJ

Lots of family picnics under our apple tree.

OAKLAND, NJ

Caught my first Rainbow trout in Ramapo River.

New York City	Thanksgiving Day Parade each year before dinner.
Bear Mountain, NY	Dad took the cub scouts on a day trip.
Glen Rock, NJ	Piano Lessons on Dad's Baby Grand Piano. No patience.

1944
TWO WEEKS AT THE JERSEY SHORE

Lavallette, NJ	Dad starts a new tradition of two weeks vacation at Ocean Beach.
Bay Head, NJ	Buying fish heads to go crapping.
Lavallette, NJ	Crabbing with fish heads and nets in Barnegat Bay
Seaside Heights, NJ	Many treats at a carnival atmosphere boardwalk on the Jersey Shore.

1945
CELEBRATING THE END OF WORLD WAR II

Union City, NJ	Grandpa took me to cliffs overlooking Hudson River to see Atlantic Fleet return from World War II.
New York Harbor	Atlantic Fleet anchored in the Hudson River is an awesome sight.
Glen Rock, NJ	Fly-over of hundreds of aircraft in formation to celebrate the end of World War II.
Glen Rock, NJ	Some aircraft tipped their wings as we waved from a deserted hilltop.

BRONX, NY	Dad took me each year to see the Red Sox / Yanks at Yankee Stadium.
UNION CITY, NJ	Remembering my Grandfather John James Roach who passed away.
GLEN ROCK, NJ	Highlight for kids was the 4th of July Parade and Central School Fair.

1946
CUB SCOUT ADVENTURES

OYSTER BAY, NY	Cub Scout trip to Long Island to see Teddy Roosevelt's Home.
WYCKOFF, NJ	Mom took us kids to Maple Lake so we could learn to swim.
NEW YORK HARBOR.	Cub Scout trip to Battleship USS Missouri where Japs surrendered.
RINGWOOD, NJ	Byrd School Trip each year to Washington's Hqs., a beautiful place.
OAKLAND, NJ	Mom's relative's cottage on Ramapo River where I did a lot of fishing.
UNION CITY, NJ	Saw the Passion Play where Mom had the lead in 1932 and met Dad.
INDIAN POINT, NY	Dad's office annual trip on Hudson River Day Line to Indian Point.
HAWTHORNE, NJ	Got a ride in a Susquehanna Railroad Diesel Engine.
HAWTHORNE, NJ	Ate too many bananas from refrigerator railroad car.

1947
YEAR OF EXPLORATION AND UNDERSTANDING

NEW YORK CITY	Dad taught me how to get to his office in New York City buy myself.
HAWTHORNE, NJ	Bobby Hohorst and I hiked to the cliffs as far as we could see.
NEW YORK CITY	Museum of Natural History, dinosaurs, whales. mummy's & more.
NEW YORK CITY	Often went alone on Erie Railroad, to subways or ferry to museums.
GLEN ROCK, NJ	Got Webelos Award for Wolf, Bear, Lion + gold and 2 silver Arrows.
NEW YORK CITY	Abigail Cronin my Great, Great Grandmother took me to the Planetarium.
GLEN ROCK, NJ	Miss Innes, gave me all "Fs" for final grades in the fifth grade.

1948
THE LOWELL THOMAS INFLUENCE

GLEN ROCK, NJ	Early TV featured world traveler, reporter Lowell Thomas.
GLEN ROCK, NJ	Exotic places like Tibet, Africa, Asia televised by Lowell Thomas.
GLEN ROCK, NJ	Easter, we got chicks, they grew up, fresh eggs every morning.
ALPINE, NJ	Picnic often with parents along Hudson River.

RIDGEWOOD, NJ	Very pretty Laura Jean Larkin was my conformation partner.
GLEN ROCK, NJ	Entered Glen Rock Junior High School and enjoyed it.
GLEN ROCK, NJ	Qualified in wood shop on dangerous lathe. Made Mom a lamp.

1949
FIRST AIRPLANE RIDE

TETEBORO, NJ	Mom hired a Bonanza Air tour over NYC for my 13th birthday.
GLEN ROCK, NJ	Saw our house from the air on this 1st airplane ride.
LINDY'S LAKE NJ	Classmate invited me for weeks vacation. I was bit by snake, but fun.
GLEN ROCK, NJ	My first painting. Copied *The Mill at Wyk*. Mom kept watercolor.
GLEN ROCK, NJ	Became newspaper boy for the *Bergen Evening Record*.
UNION CITY, NJ	Will miss my Grandpa who died. John James Roach 1873-1949

1950
INTRODUCTION TO CLASSICAL MUSIC

GLEN ROCK, NJ	Loved, Glen Rock Junior High for 7th and 8th grades.
GLEN ROCK, NJ	Mrs. Waterhouse taught me Classical Music Appreciation.

216

GLEN ROCK, NJ	Mrs. Waterhouse an outstanding teacher, great influence on my life.
BRONX, NY	Baseball at Polo Grounds. New York Giants vs. Brooklyn Dodgers.
HO-HO-KUS, NJ	Dad enrolled me in St. Luke's High School, a private Catholic School.

1951
CAPE COD TWO WEEK VACATION

DENNISPORT, MA	Dad rents cottage and we explore Cape Cod for two weeks.
HYANNISPORT. MA	While deep sea fishing, Mom caught a record, largest Blackfish.
SANDWICH, MA	Furthest from home to date. It's a big world out there.

1952
THE FIRST KISS

RIDGEWOOD, NJ	Cecilia Corcoran grabs me at # 72 bus stop and kisses me!
LAKE HOPATCONG, NJ	Sailing with Dennis Farley on his 18 foot Comet Sailboat.
HO-HO-KUS, NJ	Dislike school, have no interest, never did homework, prefer work.
RIDGEWOOD, NJ	Cecilia Corcoran starts cat fight over me. "He's mine", she says.

GLEN ROCK, NJ	First Car, 1938 Pontiac, mint condition cost $50.00 from Aunt Marian.
RIDGEWOOD, NJ	Worked at A&P supermarket as checker through high school.
SUFFERN, NY	Border town serving beer at 18 rather than 21 in New Jersey
PHILADELPHIA, PA	Took Pontiac to Independence Hall, Liberty Bell with pal Vin.
RYE BEACH, NY	Annual High School Cruise up the East River, always enjoyable.
GLEN ROCK, NJ	Became self supporting, working at A&P, bought all clothes, etc.
RIDGEWOOD, NJ	Joined Amalgamated Meat Cutters & Butchers Workman's Union.
RIDGEWOOD, NJ	Spent summer days at Graydon Pool (a lake) with friends.

TRAVELS WITH NEW JERSEY NATIONAL GUARD

RIDGEWOOD, NJ	In my 1947 Hudson Convertible, picked up Laura for school daily.
RIDGEWOOD, NJ	Escort Laura Larkin to her Cotillion at Ridgewood Country Club.
NEW YORK CITY, NY	St. Patrick's Day Parade. Green beer and St. Patrick's Cathedral.
TEANECK, NJ	Joined the NJ National Guard at age 18. Gung ho for travel!
KINGSTON, CANADA.	First trip to another country, Canada, from Camp Drum NY.
1000 ISLANDS, NY	Visit the 1,000 Islands on ST. Lawrence River with National Guard.
WATERTOWN, NY	First Pullman Sleeping Car overnight on New York Central to Teaneck.
TEANECK, NJ	First formal Military Ball at Teaneck Armory, NJ National Guard.
WHIPPANY, NJ	Tommy Dorsey Orchestra at Meadowbrook Nite Club for Junior Prom.
BROOKLYN, NY	Visited Coney Island often, loved parachute jump and roller coaster.
RIDGEWOOD, NJ	Played end on St. Luke's Soccer Team and beat Ridgewood High.
NEWARK, NJ	Played hooky often to see constellations take off at Newark Airport.

GRADUATED FROM ST. LUKE'S HIGH SCHOOL

HO-HO-KUS, NJ	I was in the Senior Play titled, *More than Meets the Eye.*
WASHINGTON, DC	Class trip with 6 classmates to our nations capital. A fun trip.
WASHINGTON, DC	Tour of White House, Ford's Theatre, Lincoln Memorial et al.
WASHINGTON, DC	Cherry Blossoms in bloom, Toured capital building and congress.
MONT VERNON, VA	George Washington's Home on Potomac River.
ALEXANDRIA, VA	Lees Home and Arlington Cemetery.
HO-HO-KUS, NJ	Won many St. Luke's Dance Contests with sweetheart Joyce Borell.
WHIPPANY, NJ	Theresa Brewer entertains at the Meadowbrook Nite Club.
GLEN ROCK, NJ	Joyce's parents finally allow her to ride in my car.
HO-HO-KUS, NJ	Received School Spirit Award at graduation ceremony.
COLCHESTER, VT	Became Freshman at St. Michael's College in September.
TICONDEROGA, NY	Harrison Scott invites me for weekend to visit fort and go hunting.
TICONDEROGA, NY	Learned full history of Fort Ticonderoga.
CROWN POINT, NY	Toured the redoubts of Crown Point from the French & Indian War.
BURLINGTON, VT	Second Formal Military Ball with the Vermont National Guard.

ST. MICHAEL'S COLLEGE

COLCHESTER, VT	After tryouts, made the ski team, track team and x-country team.
BURLINGTON, VT	First ski jump was 30 meter jump at University of Vermont.
HANOVER, NH	Compete with Dartmouth College at their ski bowl.
SARANAC LAKE, NY	I came in last on the x-county skiing competition with six colleges.
LYNDONVILLE, VT	Burke Mountain Ski Trip. Stayed at Darling Inn. Great!
HANOVER, NH	Amazed at Jose Clemente Orozco Mural on Dartmouth Library Walls.
BURLINGTON, VT	Worked as a waiter at Sugar House and Park Café.
COLCHESTER, VT	Flunked out of SMC with three As, Physics, Philosophy, Humanities, and three Fs, Math, French and Religion. Mostly not interested.
COLCHESTER, VT	Enjoyed Greek Literature of Homer, Plato, Aristotle, & Tragedies.
SOUTH ORANGE, NJ	Enrolled as a Philosophy Major at Seton Hall University
NEW YORK CITY, NY	Joe King's Rathskeller, a college hangout. Took Laura Larkin.

1957

SETON HALL UNIVERSITY

SOUTH ORANGE, NJ	Got all As, in Logic, Epistemology, Metaphysics, Cosmology and Rational Psychology.
KIAMESHA LAKE, NY	Worked a Borscht Belt waiter job at Kiamesha Lodge for the summer.
MONTICELLO, NY	At the Concord Hotel next door I met Buster Crabbe (Flash Gordon).
MONTICELLO, NY	Jewish father from Bronx pleaded that I not date his daughter.
COLCHESTER, VT	Re-entered St. Michaels college as a Junior. Didn't miss a beat.
GLEN ROCK, NJ	Ayn Rand. Read all her books, *Atlas Shrugged* influenced me.

1958
FRANCHI CONSTRUCTION COMPANY

Saranac Lake, NY	As leader of SMC Band we were invited to concert in Saranac Lake NY.
Evansville, IN	Six of us traveled to Evansville to cheer SMC Team at the NCAA Finals.
Indianapolis, IN	Saw the famed Indianapolis Speedway on the way to Evansville.
Covington, KY	Stopped across river from Cincinnati on return trip from NCAA Finals.
Winooski, VT	Met Jacqueline Frenette and asked her to dance while on crutches.
Colchester, VT	Junior Weekend, Les Elgart Orchestra. I took Jacqueline Frenette.
Colchester, VT	Jackie and I were always seen together at college functions.
Burlington, VT	Hired as Office Manager of Franchi Construction Co., by Mr. Ibey.
West Newton, MA	Travel to HQ of Franchi Construction Co., to learn Office Management
Winooski, VT	Dated Jacqueline Frenette throughout school year and summer.
Burlington, VT	Rented apartment on top floor at Church and Main with great views.
Winooski, VT	Stella Frenette with 10 children treated me like her eleventh.
Winooski, VT	Stella had one of her daughters deliver lunch to me daily at work.

BURLINGTON, VT	Dad visits me and suggests I quit Franchi and seek job in New Jersey.
PARAMUS, NJ	With impeccable credentials from Mr. Ibey I landed a very good job.
PARAMUS, NJ	ITT, Federal Electric Company offered me the job of Manager of DEWLine Technical Libraries with 71 branch Libraries across Arctic.
GLEN ROCK, NJ	Lived with parents, paid board and commuted to Vermont on weekends to see Jackie.
TEANECK, NJ	Enrolled in Farleigh Dickenson University as Psychology major.
GLEN ROCK, NJ	Bought at 1952 Cadillac Convertible, powder blue with white top.
BURLINGTON, VT	Visited Jackie at least every second weekend. 700 miles round trip.
ROME, NY	Second Business trip. Flew to Griffis AFB with rank of major at BOQ.
PARAMUS, NJ	Received Top Secret Clearance from US Government.
TARRYTOWN, NY	Mom and Dad's 25th Anniversary held at Patricia Murphy's

ALASKA TRIP AND MARRIAGE

ANCHORAGE, ALASKA	Touring Alaska's largest city of 40,000 population in 1959.
DENALI NAT. PARK	At 20,000 feet you look up out window to Mt. McKinley .
FAIRBANKS, ALASKA	Bonfire remnants from statehood celebration still on Main Street.
FAIRBANKS, ALASKA	Skied University of Alaska Ski Bowl. Saw their stuffed Kodiak Bear.
ARCTIC CIRCLE, ALASKA	Got my Crossing Arctic Circle Certificate from Wein Alaska Airlines.
KOBUK VALLEY NAT PARK	Herds of caribou seen running across tundra from airplane.
POINT BARROW, ALASKA	Northernmost spot in North America. Visited Eskimo Village.
POINT BARROW, ALASKA	Visited Top of the World Hotel and stayed at DEWLine Main Site.
POINT BARROW, ALASKA	Located Will Rogers and Wiley Post Monument.
GATES ARCTIC NAT. PARK	The formidable Brooks Ranges separates tundra and Arctic Ocean.
BARTER ISLAND, ALASKA	500 Miles east is another DEWLine Main site with Eskimo Village.
WHITEHORSE, CANADA	Visited by Pan Am Clipper in the Yukon Territory of Canada.
KETCHIKAN, ALASKA	A small fishing village accessible by boat or plane.

JUNEAU, ALASKA	Alaska's Capital, last stop on Pan Am Clipper before Seattle.
WINOOSKI, VT	Married Jacqueline Frenette in St. Francis Church, Thanksgiving Day.
COLCHESTER, VT	Wedding reception at Sunny Hollow.
MONTREAL, CANADA	Queen Elizabeth Hotel, for the first night of honeymoon.
QUEBEC CITY CANADA	Honeymoon at Chateau Frontenac, Quebec City.

1960
OUR FIRST YEAR TOGETHER

HAWTHORNE, NJ	We rented our brand new one bedroom apartment.
NEW YORK CITY	Benny Goodman Concert, Rainbow Room, Top Floor RCA Building.
PARAMUS, NJ	Changed jobs to System Development Corporation a month vacation.
PARAMUS, NJ	Invented, designed and installed the SATIRE System.
MONTGOMERY, NY	Sports car race with Al and Roe Gotthardt.
FORT DIX, NJ	Saw night demonstration of company fire power with tracer bullets.
LAVALLETTE, NJ	Rented Cottage at Ocean Beach for a week's vacation.
SPRING LAKE, NJ	Golf with Dad at Spring Lake Country Club.
SEASIDE HEIGHTS, NJ	Weekends at a B&B near the beach and boardwalk.
PHILADELPHIA, PA	Veterans Stadium to see Giants vs. Eagles with Jackie's brother Ray.
SEA GIRT, NJ	Officer candidate School with New Jersey National Guard.
JACKSONBERG, NJ	Deer hunting on the banks of the Delaware River.
VINELAND, NJ	Sports car races with Al and Rose.
HAWTHORNE, NJ	Read all of Taylor Caldwell's books, Liked *Dear and Glorious Physician*.

CONVENTION SPEAKER

Washington, DC	Sheraton Park Hotel, SLA Convention Speaker, SATIRE Presentation.
Washington, DC	A week at the Sheraton Park to show Jackie all the historic sites.
Limerock, CT	Took my little brother Jimmy to his first National Sports Car Race.
Warwick, NY	First Home built 3br, 2 baths, at 32 Sunset Terrace, Warwick, NY
Lexington, MA	Stayed at Battle Creek Inn, paid by company at this historic site.
Concord, MA	Shots heard round the world, starts revolutionary war.
Cumberland, WV	National Sports Car Race in West Virginia, just Jackie and I alone.
Valley Forge, PA	George Washington's winter camp, before crossing the Delaware.
Atlantic City, NJ	Walked the Boardwalk with Al and Rose. Clairidge Hotel Casino.
New York City	Spartacus Broadway opening at Radio City Music Hall.
Mystic, CT	Mystic Seaport for a nice trip with Al and Rose.
Princeton, NJ	NY Giants & Eagles Pre-season Football at Princeton with Al and Rose.
Warwick, NY	Completed reading all John Steinbeck's books to date.

1962
FLORIDA, CALIFORNIA & CHICAGO

SANTA MONICA, CA	SDC HQ in Santa Monica wanted SATIRE presentations for scientists.
MALIBU, CA	Met Charles Bronson sitting alone at Bar. We talked until closing.
WARWICK, NY	First new car a 1962 Volvo 4dr sedan, black.
HOLLYWOOD, FL	SATIRE presentation at Diplomat Hotel Convention Center.
ST. AUGUSTINE, FL	Elected to drive to Florida to see southern states
SAVANNAH, GA	The Pirate House for Southern Fried Chicken. Pretty good too.
MIAMI, BEACH, FL	The Fontainebleau Hotel, fancy restaurants, entertainment, beaches.
FT. LAUDERDALE, FL	Patricia Murphy's for cocktails and dining and Bahia Mar Yacht Club.
HOLLYWOOD, FL	Ten days all expense paid vacation for a 1 hour SATIRE presentation.
SANTA MONICA, CA	Many trips to Santa Monica, stayed at Miramar and Oceana Hotels.
CHICAGO, IL	SATIRE presentation at ADI Convention, Pick Congress Hotel.
NIAGRA FALLS, NY	Elected to drive to Chicago to see Niagara Falls on the way.
CHICAGO, IL	Ten Days all expense vacation for making one hour presentation.

CHICAGO, IL	Restaurants include, The Berghof, Italian Village, The Bakery.
WARWICK, NY	Elected President of the Wickham Village Homowners. 350 Homes.
WARWICK, NY	Enjoyed John Steinbeck's newest book, *Travels With Charlie*.

RIDGEWOOD, NJ	Our daughter Patricia Ann Roach is born 3/12/63 at Valley Hospital.
ACADIA NAT. PARK	Maine. Our first national Park inspires us to visit them all.
ACADIA NAT. PARK	Water is ice old on the coast of Maine.
BAR HARBOR, ME	Embark on Bluenose for voyage to Nova Scotia. Got seasick.
LONDON, NOVA SCOTIA	Stayed in B&B, noticed memorial to British defeating Americans.
HALIFAX, NOVA SCOTIA	Bars closed to women, found out the hard way. Visit fortress.
CHARLOTTETOWN. PEI	Federation Hall where Canada was formed.
CAVINDISH, PEI	Spent a week in rented cottage on beautiful beach. Warm water.
CAVINDISH, PEI	Swimming in the Gulf of St. Lawrence. Read all Kenneth Roberts books. Favorites, *Oliver Wiswell* and *Rabble in Arms.*
ST. JOHN, NB	Bay of Fundy, highest tides in the world. Tidal bore on river.
FREDRICKTON, NB	Worlds longest wooden covered bridge. Crossed it in Volvo.
MADAWASKA, ME	The very northern tip of Maine. Potato country *Travels With Charlie.*
RIVEIRE DU-LOUPE, PQ	Small French Canadian town on wide part of St. Lawrence River.

QUEBEC CITY, CANADA	Chateaux Frontenac. Our 2nd visit to this beautiful hotel.
DOTHAN, AL	Ft. Rucker Alabama installs SATIRE System for Combat Dev. Command
ENTERPRISE, AL	Peanut farms, boiled nuts, Catfish Row like Main Street.
MANASSAS, VA	Toured this Civil War battlefield.
SANTA MONICA, CA	SATIRE full page ads in *Scientific American* & *Science & Technology*.

1964
EARLY TRIPS TO CALIFORNIA

SANTA MONICA, CA	Considered a move to California, but too expensive.
HYDE PARK, NY	Visited both Roosevelt and Vanderbuilt estates on Hudson River.
FLATBUSH, NY	First visit to Shea Stadium to see Mets vs. Dodgers baseball.
SANTA MONICA, CA	Stayed at Miramir Hotel, met Joseph Cotton, enjoyed Mai Tai's.
SAN JOSE, CA	Invited to make SATIRE presentation to IBM Scientists.
SAN JOSE, CA	Receive unsolicited job offer from IBM with 20% increase in pay.
SAN JOSE, CA	Accept IBM job offer to work near home in Yorktown Heights NY.
PEEKSKILL, NY	Cross Hudson River on Bear Mountain Bridge to get to work daily.
NEW YORK CITY, NY	Many weeks at NYU Law Library to design legal system for lawyers.
NEW YORK CITY, NY	Found Katz's Deli one of the best Jewish Deli's in the US. Go often!
WARWICK, NY	Ernest hemingway. Read all his published works to date.

KINGSTON, NY	IBM offers transfer to Kingston NY Manufacturing 360 Conputer.
HURLEY, NY	IBM buys my home in Warwick, NY so I option home in Hurley, NY.
SAN FRANCISCO, CA	Took Jackie on her first trip to California. Stayed at Mark Hopkins.
SAN FRANCISCO, CA	Dinner at the Top of the Mark. George Liberace entertains.
YOSEMITE, NAT. PK.	Our 2nd National Park, yet one of the most beautiful scenes in US.
SEQUOIA, NAT PK.	Giant Sequoias older than the birth of Christ. We drove through one.
KINGS CANYON, NP	We can get used to this,. The national Parks are very nice.
SAN FRANCISCO, CA	Open Jaw flight to Hawaii, return to San Diego.
WAKIKI BEACH, HI	A weeks vacation at Hilton Hawaiian Village at age 29, Jackie 23.
WAKIKI BEACH, HI	Richard Boon invites us to his table for an afternoon of cocktails.
WAKIKI BEACH, HI	Luau with Hawaiian dancers with Diamond Head in background.
LA JOLLA, CA	Our first trip to this beautiful place. This is where I want to retire.
LA JOLLA, CA	You are talking retirement at age 29? Either La Jolla or San Diego.

SAN DIEGO, CA	La Jolla is a small community of San Diego, both are wonderful.
SAN DIEGO, CA	We stayed at the El Cortez Hotel the tallest building in San Diego.
SAN DIEGO, CA	Dinning and dancing on the top floor of El Cortez with city below.
KINGSTON, NY	The Dugout, Skytop, Rathskeller, & Deane's in Woodstock, favorites.
HURLEY, NY	Boris Pasternak's book, *Doctor Zhivago*, changed my direction in life.

COLORADO VACATION

DENVER, CO	We took our daughter, age 3 on her first flight for aweek in Colorado.
CENTRAL CITY, CO	The Teller House Saloon, has the Face on the Baroom Floor.
CENTRAL CITY, CO	A historic gold mining town with a working Opera House.
ROCKY MOUNTAIN, NP	Roger Frenette gave us a tour of Rocky Mountain National Park.
CHEYANNE, WY	Frontier Days Celebration with lots of cowboys, rodeo and beer.
MIDDLETOWN, NY	Our son Michael Sean Roach born 12/9/66 Middletown Hospital.
HURLEY, NY	Russian Literature captivated me, Tolstoy, Dostiekvsky, Turgenev.

FIRST CRUISESHIP EXPERIENCE

CURACAO, NA	Flew to Netherlands Antilles for Chandris Cruise Line, (now Celebrity)
CURACAO, NA	Embark on Chandris Cruise Line SS Regina bond for Jamaica.
CURACAO, NA	Met Bill and Helena Philips from IBM who became good friends.
KINGSTON, JAMICA	Cocktails at the Jamaica Hilton caused us to almost miss the ship.
KINGSTON, JAMICA	People on board cheering as we ran down the dock late to board.
FREEPORT, BAHAMAS	Stayed 3 days at the Kings Inn, talked to Walter Cronkite, did Limbo.
FREEPORT, BAHAMAS	Princess Resort & Casino was preferred to Lucadia Casinos.
NASSAU, BAHAMAS	Arrived on Easter Sunday, everything closed. Swim, Sheraton Beach.
BURLINGTON, VT	Opened first business, *Burlington Speedway*, model car racing center.
HURLEY, NY	Contemplated and wrote thoughts on *Dynamism.*
MONTREAL, CANADA	Expo 67 Worlds Fair a great experience. Mona Lisa on tour.
MALLETS BAY, VT	Rented cottage at Sadie's to spend week at Expo 67. Took Kids.
KINGSTON, NY	Spent many weekends with Bill and Helena at Williams Lake.

BERMUDA

BERMUDA	Weeks vacation at Mermaid Beach Resort with Bill & Helena Phillips.
BERMUDA	Did motorbike tour of Island with Bill and Helena.
BERMUDA	Bill Philips and I played golf an world famous Mid-Ocean Golf Course.
CATSKILL, NY	Took kids to Catskill Game Farm and dinner on Hudson River.
WOODSTOCK, NY	Played golf with Fred Ritchel at Woodstock Country Club.
ARMONK, NY	Offered job at IBM Headquarters in Armonk, NY causing me to move.
WALDWICK, NJ	Took option on home to work across Hudson River at IBM HQ.
NEW YORK CITY, NY	Took kids often to Met Museum of Art to learn about Impressionists.
NEW YORK CITY, NY	Winning contestants on ABC's baby Game, won $1,500. In prizes.
NEW YORK CITY, NY	Sardi's after our TV win. Sammy Davis Jr. & Vincent Price next table.
WALDWICK, NJ	Lived only 8 miles from NYC, took advantage of many Broadway Plays.
NEW YORK CITY, NY	*How to Suceed in Business Withour Really Trying,* staring Michele Lee.
NEW YORK CITY, NY	Broadway play, *Any Wednesday* staring Sandy Dennis.

NEW YORK CITY, NY	Two regrets; Never met Jackie Gleason my favorite personality at Toot Shores or Maria Callas, at the MET, the greatest Diva ever!
GREENWICH, CT	Kathie MacHale gave me tour of her affluent home town near IBM.
WALDWICK, NJ	By-Line Ernest Hemingway p. 186 & 281 list his recommended books.
WALDWICK, NJ	Who is he kidding? None as good as, *Old man and the Sea.*

MAKING THE MOST OF PROXIMATEY TO NEW YORK CITY

New York City, NY	Met Lee Remick personally for autograph in her dressing room after Broadway play *Wait Until Dark.*
White Plains, NY	Kathie McHale helps pick out frame for Chabas, *September Morn.*
Flushing, NY	Worlds Fair in New York, saw the *Pieata* by Michaelangelo. Beauiful!
Dothan, Al	Sold SATIRE SYSTEM to US Army Combat Development Command.
Huntsville, AL	Tour of Huntsville Space Center with rockets and space capsules.
Birmingham, AL	Top of 21 Colony Restaurant, for a good time in Birmingham.
White Plains, NY	Good friends Kathy McHale and John Derby get married.
White Plains, NY	The Derby's great wedding & reception at Maxell's Beer Garden.
New York City, NY	Saw Broadway Play, *Hair* the night before opening. Predict success.
Boston, MA	Boston Museum of Art. Dinner at Café Budapest.
New York City, NY	*Russian Tea Room, Luchow's, Mama Leone's* all favorities.
Toronto, Canada	*Ed's Warehouse* on Waterront. Young Street worth a walk.
New York City, NY	Met Johnny Carson on elevator at Americana Hotel.

NEW YORK CITY, NY	Friends hired Johnnny Carson's limo driver to take me out.
NEW YORK CITY, NY	*Copacabana Club, Forvum of the 12 Caesars, Riverboat Lounge.*
SADDLE RIVER, NJ	Pumpkin Patch, Introduce Kathie and John Derby to my parents.
NEW YORK CITY, NY	MET Museum of Art. Lobby has Chabas *September Morn*, Awesome.
WHITE PLAINS, NY	Predict song *Goin Out of My Head* will last a very long time.
NEW YORK CITY, NY	Took kids often to Greenwich Village and fancy restaurants.
WHITE PLAINS, NY	While working for IBM I wrote the poem, *The Purpose of Life.*
ESSEX JUNCTION, VT	IBM Transfer from IBM HQ Armonk NY to IBM Burlington, VT.
COLCHESTER, VT	Bought house and moved in December. No traffic, just cows.
COLCHESTER, VT	Hemingway's posthumous book, *Moveable Feast* a major influence on me.

MY YEAR AS AN ARCHITECT

BURLINGTON, VT	First opera, *Marriage of Figero*, sung in English. Awful! A Mistake that turned me off opera for more than 20 years. Get me outta here!
MONTREAL, CANADA	Montreal Canadians v Boston . Got Jean Belaveau's autograph.
NEW YORK CITY, NY	Met John & Kathie Derby for *Man of La Mancha* & Playboy Club.
BURLINGTON, VT	Shakespear Festivel, *King Lear*, University of Vermont.
SHELBURNE, VT	Museum has one of 3 Degas *La Petite Dancer de quartorse ans.*
MONTREAL, CANADA	NY Giants lose to Steelers in exhibitition game. Sherman fired.
COLCHESTER, VT	Kathie & John Derby visit our home before moving to Florida.
BURLINGTON, VT	Enrolled in Power Squadron to learn boating rules of the road.
WILLISTON, VT	Rocky Ridge Country Club, hole in one by Ray Frenette.
WATERBURY, VT	interlude.
STOWE, VT	One week ski vacation with ski lessons for our two kids.
JEFFERSONVILLE, VT	Took kids often to learn to improve skiing a Madonna Mountain.
ESSEX JUNCTION, VT	Article in IBM Magazine concerning my work. Information Science.

COLCHESTER, VT

Bought land on a cliff with view of Lake for new home I designed.

BURLINGTON, VT

Spoon River Anthology, by Edgar Lee Masters, a wonderful play.

ESSEX JUNCTION, VT

Promoted to Manager, Laboratory Information Systems at IBM.

COLCHESTER, VT

Spent most of year in architecture designing new home for four.

VERMONT SKI VACATIONS WITH KIDS

COLCHESTER, VT	Explained with music *Man of La Mancha*, to my daughter Patty.
BURLINGTON, VT	Ray Charles in Concert at memorial Auditorium, just great!
BOLTON VALLEY, VT	My first TV Production on Information Science. Hired Vermont ETV.
SUGARBUSH, VT	Second year vacation for kids to take ski lessons, this time Sugarbush.
SUGARBUSH, VT	*Common Man Restaurant* a favorite. Rack of Lamb or Steak au Poivre.
WAITSFIELD, VT	Kids prefer Sugarbush to Mad River Glen.
BOLTON VALLEY, VT	Night skiing at Bolton Valley Lodge.
MONTGOMERY, VT	Jay Peak has a giant cable car to the top of the mountain.
MONTGOMERY, VT	*Zack's On The Rocks* is a dining experience you will not forget.
WAITSFIELD, VT	Took kids to Glen Ellen skiing for variety.
WATERBURY, VT	Interlude has lasted a full year. Details in book, *Serial Monogamy*.
COLCHESTER, VT	Enjoyed James Michener's books, *Hawaii*, *The Source* and *Caravans*.
QUEBEC, CANADA	Ski weekend at Mt. Tremblant.

1972

WATERBURY, VT	Interlude destined to failure ends, I see a psychiatrist for 6 weeks.
BURLINGTON, VT	Take up Oil Painting in a class in Burlington.
BURLINGTON, VT	The elderly professional psychiatrist guided me out of depression.
KENNEBUNKPORT ME	All the lobster you can eat. Mike doesn't like MacDonald's anymore.
BURLINGTON, VT	Completed *The Dead Oak Protects*, my first Impressionist painting.
COLCHESTER, VT	Helping Patty qualify for Girl Scout Merit Badges. She has so many.
BURLINGTON, VT	Completed *Interlude* in the Degas style of Realism with a palate knife.
CHARLOTTE, VT	Took sailing lessons with Neil Fisher's Sailing School.
BURLINGTON, VT	Completed *State of My Mind* my first surrealistic painting.
BURLINGTON, VT	Broadway play, *Up With People* rejuvenated my positive outlook.
BURLINGTON, VT	Completed *Sunflowers*, reaching for the sun, now owned by Patty.

FIRST TRIP TO EUROPE

PARIS, FRANCE	Jackie and I arrived in Paris from Montreal on Air France.
PARIS, FRANCE	A full week in Paris paid for by IBM with another week in Germany.
PARIS, FRANCE	Total immersion, stayed a week at French, Hotel Gare de Lyon.
ESSONNES, FRANCE	Train from Gare de Leon Paris to IBM Essonnes on IBM Business.
ESSONNES, FRANCE	First IBM facility that I noticed wine served in cafeteria. Relaxing.
PARIS, FRANCE	Louvre, created by Napoleon, saw *Winged Victory, Mona Lisa* et al.
PARIS, FRANCE	Jeu de Paume (Gatehouse) contains impressionist paintings in 1973.
PARIS FRANCE	Favorite painting, *Absinthe* by Degas adorns a wall in Jeu de Paume.
PARIS, FRANCE	Favorite sculpture. *Little Dancer Age 14* is also in Jeu de Paume.
PARIS, FRANCE	Champs Elysses cafes between Arch de Triumph, Place de Concorde.
PARIS FRANCE	Eiffel Tower, good views from top, dined at *Le Trois Mutton.*
PARIS FRANCE	Favorite Restaurant, *Au Pied du Cachon,* (At the Foot of the Pig).
VERSAILLE, FRANCE	Palace of Versailles represents living in excess before revolution.

SWITZERLAND	Grindenwald. Stayed in a beautiful Swiss Chalet for weekend in Alps.
SWITZERLAND	Jungfrau means young virgin. The Ice palace at top is worth a visit.
SWITZERLAND	Interlaken. Tour Lake Lucerne by car on the way to Zurich.
SWITZERLAND	Zurich. A fine city with beer gardens and cafes around Lake Zurich.
STUTTGART, GERMANY	Stayed in German Hotel as English is the Language of Technology.
STUTTGART, GERMANY	Dinner atop the Fernsatrum, the tallest point in Stuttgart, a TV Tower.
STUTTGART, GERMANY	Toured the nearby Black Forest consisting of many small towns.
MAINZ, GERMANY	Stayed at the Mainz Hilton on the banks of the Rhine River.
FRANKFORT, GERMANY	First class European Sleeping Car overnight to Hannover.
HANNOVER, GERMANY	This city was leveled by bombing in World War II, Now rebuilt modern.
MADRID, SPAIN	The Prado Gallery, contains works of El Greco, Valazquez and Goya.
MADRID, SPAIN	Circular French Fries? I finally realized were squid, today's Calamiri.
TORREMOLINOS, SPAIN	Read Michener's book *The Drifter's*. Had to see this place for myself.
TORREMOLINOS, SPAIN	Stayed at Holiday Inn Beachfront to swim in the Mediterranean.
MALAGA, SPAIN	Gaucho dinner and festival for an evening of Spanish entertainment.

MONTREAL, CANADA	Return to New York on Iberia Airlines with flight to Burlington VT.
CAPE COD, MA	Took kids tenting for a week on Cape Cod National Seashore.
COLCHESTER, VT	Second Business Venture, Bay Harbor Yachts, Ltd.
PROVINCETOWN, MA	Took kids on Schooner Sail in Atlantic Ocean.
BURLINGTON, VT	Invited to join the Ethan Allen Club, a gentlemen's club.
PLYMOUTH, MA	Took kids to see Pilgrims Plymouth Rock & Old Ironsides warship.

1974
TORTOLA

ST. CROIX	Combined IBM Business Trip to St. Croix with week in Tortola.
SR. CROIX	Women found beheaded on beach, hotels empty, left same day.
TORTOLA, BVI	Seaplane to St. Thomas, Bomba Charger to Tortola
TORTOLA, BVI	Stayed at Long Bay Resort. A Paradise, met Bob and Joan Bailey.
TORTOLA, BVI	Spectacular Long Bay Beach, We all agreed to come again next year.
ST. THOMAS	Pineapple Beach Resort. A letdown compared to Long Bay Resort.
SAN JUAN, PR	Stayed at Caribe Hilton, enjoyed their casino and beach.
SAN JUAN PR	Tour Old Town where we had our first Spanish dinner, Piaia. Great!
NEW ORLEANS, LA	Jazz on Bourbon Street, dinner at *Antoine's* breakfast at *Brennen's*.
CLEARWATER BEACH, FL	Stayed at Holiday Inn Beachfront to visit John & Kathie Derby.
TAMPA, FL	Top Ten Spanish, The *Columbia Restaurant* in Yarbor City was great.
LUTZ, FL	Visit John & Kathie Derby gave them tree for front yard.
TARPON SPRINGS, FL	Heard so much about *Pappas Greek Restaurant*. Had to dine there.

SAILING THE BRITISH VIRGIN ISLANDS

ROADTOWN, TORTOLA	Chartered Out Island 41 Ketch provisioned for 3 couples.
NORMAN ISLAND, BVI	Caves to explore, Lots of good cooking with Jackie, Joan and Linda.
VIRGIN GORDA, BVI	Swimming at the Baths, a most unusual place with crystal clear water.
VIRGIN GORDA, BVI	Dinner at Bitter End Yacht Club.
TORTOLA, BVI	Pristine Cane Garden Bay. Crabs at Stanley's. Joan practiced ballet.
JOST VAN DYKE, BVI	Black Bart's was closed. Had dinner & dominos with native family.
PETER ISLAND, BVI	Dining & dancing at *Peter Island Rocky Resort* on our last evening.
TORTOLA, BVI	Apres Cruise, spent a few days at Long Bay Resort, our favorite.
MONTREAL, CANADA	Two weeks at Place Boneventure, for Boat Show. Restaurants galore.
ORWELL, VT	Ended 16 year marriage. 8/1/75
SHELBURNE, VT	Had a private mooring at Lake Champlain Yacht Club.
NORTH HERO, VT	Opened Marina Internationale, that I designed, financed and built.
COLCHESTER, VT	Daughter, Patty, painted Don Quixote's horse, *Rocinante* on transom.

1976
THE GREEK ISLANDS

Colchester, VT	Married 3rd wife Micheline Trembly aboard 4 rafted yachts 5/4/76.
Shelburne, VT	Reception at Café Shelburne, off the menu. Owners, Andre & Daniel.
Mykonos, Greece	Windmills and alleys. Romantic B&B overlooked picturesque harbor.
Mykonos, Greece	Matina Athanasopoulov owns the B&B. Told her I would return.
Athens Greece	Birthplace of Democracy. Walked the Acropolis. A beautiful city.
Athens, Greece	The Plaka has great food. Temple of Athena Nike 426BC
Sounion, Greece	Temple of Poisidon on cliff overlooking Aegean Sea. Saw no nymphs.
Epidavros, Greece	Amphitheatre, whisper at center, be heard in top row. Built 4 BC.
Corinth, Greece	Site of the Temple of Apollo and the hand dug Corinth Canal.
Athens, Greece	Parthenon, 447 BC, impressive Doric Architecture.
Delos, Greece	Mykonos was best island, will return someday.
Mallets Bay, VT	Delivery of my new S2 30 foot yacht, diesel with hot shower.
Camel's Hump, VT	Took kids mountain climbing to top of Camel's Hump.

SARATOGA, NY	Day at historic Saratoga Race Track with Lee Faucet. Fun but no win.
BURTON ISLAND, VT	Took kids to Burton Island on new 30' yacht *Rocinante* for 3 days.
HOLLAND, MI	Weeks vacation at Point West Yacht Club on Lake Michigan.
VALCOUR ISLAND, NY	Sailed with kids to see this historic site of the battle of Valcour 1776.
BURLINGTON, VT	Picked up Mike every Saturday for his St. Marks bowling league.
TORTOLA, BVI	Returned again and met Jack Baxter MD, who became a close friend.

Nevis	A weeks vacation seeking adventure beyond favorite Tortola.
Nevis	Remote Island, no direct flights, no brewed coffee, yet nice.
Nevis	Stayed at Pinney's Beach Resort. Dinner with Nevis Governor.
Nevis	Birthplace of Alexander Hamilton. Explored entire island
St. Kitts	Took ferry with natives and cows to this more developed island.
St. Kitts	Visited Brimstone Hill Fortress the Gibralter of the Caribbean.
St. Kitts	Toured Island. Lots of sugar cane and a few many big hotels.
Nevis	Breakfast with couple making landfall from Europe in 30' sailboat.
Montreal, Canada	Two weeks at Place Boneventure with 13 yachts in boat show.
Burlington, VT	Broadway Play *Equus* at Memorial Auditorium.
Lake Champlain, VT	Week long sail with kids exploring Lake Champlain.
Shelburne, VT	Dinner with kids at Café Shelburne. Rocinante at Shelburne mooring.
Ferrisburg, VT	Anchored with kids in Arnold Bay, where Ben Arnold torched ship.
Essex, NY	Cooked dinner on board. Kids loved breakfast at quaint Essex Café.

TICONDEROGA, NY	Anchored below fort and rowed ashore to tour fort. Awesome!
VERGENNES, VT	Anchored overnight at Basin Harbor Club for a family dinner.
PARTRIDGE COVE, NY	Most beautiful cove on Lake Champlain, Mike went fishing.
WILLSBORO, NY	Our last evening with kids at Marina before returning to Malletts Bay.
NEWPORT, RI	Stayed at Sheraton Newport to attend Newport Show.
MINNEAPOLIS, MN	Visit to Micheline's sister and did boat ride on Mississippi River.
CHICOUTIMI, CANADA	Laurintide National Park en-route to visit Micheline's family.
BALTIMORE, MD	*Café des Artists*, a French Restaurant that made our day in Baltimore.
ANNAPOLIS, MD	Sailing the Chesapeake Bay on an S2 36 yacht on a sunny day.
VIRGINIA BEACH, VA	Stayed at Holiday Inn Oceanfront to experience this fine beach.
WILLIAMSBURG, VA	Replica Colonial Village serves colonial foods and brew in pubs.
ESSEX JUNCTION, VT	Completed professional paper on *Palladium Depletion*.
CHICAGO, IL	Attended Chicago Boat Show at McCormack Place.
CHICAGO, IL	*The Bakery* for Beef Wellington and *Cape Cod Room* are favorites.
NORTH HERO, VT	Purchased 2800 feet of lakefront on 14 acres to develop a marina.
NORTH HERO, VT	New Lakefront Home purchased at Five Oaks, Savage Point.

1978
DISNEY WORLD WITH KIDS

ORLANDO, FL	First time for Patty and Michael was so enjoyable and unforgettable.
CLEARWATER, FL	We stayed on an S2 30 Yacht at Clearwater Beach Marina.
CLEARWATER, FL	Deep Sea Fishing on party boat with my son Mike.
BOSTON, MA	Dinners at *Loke Ober* Steakhouse and *Jimmy's Harbor Side.* Gourmet!
NEW HAVEN, VT	Oktoberfest, Vermont's largest and quite an event.
MIDDLEBURY, VT	*Mr. Up's,* offers outdoor dining on their deck overlooking Otter River.
CLEARWATER, FL	Second week with Lothar and Collette on S2 Yacht. Cold both times.
TAMPA, FL	Dinner with long time friends, John and Kathie Derby.

1979
BIG RED MURPHY OF FIVE OAKS

North Hero, VT	Vermont Governor's wife offers me pick of the litter, Irish Setters.
North Hero, VT	Tiny red 8 inch pedigree puppy I named for his address.
North Hero, VT	Neighbors love Murphy and insist I allow him to run loose.
Montreal, Canada	Another two weeks, this time at Chateau Champlain.
Montreal, Canada	Patty chose the *Symposium* with Greek dancing for her birthday.
North Hero, VT	Second wife diagnosed with cancer trying holistic cure.
Point Clair, Canada	Invited to dinner at Point Clair Yacht Club. Impressive.
Sorel, Canada	Sailed Rocinante the length of Richelieu River.
Montreal, Canada	Sailed Rocinante from Sorel to Montreal on St. Lawrence River.
Montreal, Canada	In the water Boat Show, saves trucking yachts to show.
North Hero, VT	Second wife visits with husband and lost weight and looks fragile.
North Hero, VT	Micheline agrees to accompany her to Tijuana, Mexico treatment.

TORTOLA, BVI	Treated my parents to 10 days at Long Bay Resort, Oceanfront.
ST. JOHN, VI	Took parents to Caneel Bay Plantation. Mom loved private beach.
ST. JOHN, VI	Virgin Islands Underwater National Park. Lots of pretty fish.
MONTREAL, CANADA	My brother Jimmy set up entire Boat Show at Place Boneventure.
SOREL, CANADA	Second cruise up Richelieu River with two S2 30 Yachts to Montreal.
LAC ST. JEAN, CANADA	Took kids on a week trout fishing north of Lac St. Jean, Quebec.
BURLINGTON, VT	Bought tickets for Micheline to accompany 2nd wife to San Diego, CA
BURLINGTON, VT	Micheline and 2nd wife board plane for treatment in Tijuana, Mexico.
NORTH HERO, VT	Divorce 3rd wife Micheline.
NEW YORK CITY, NY	Stayed at Americana Hotel. Took date to Broadway Play, *Tintypes*.
NEW YORK CITY, NY	Dinner at *Windows of the World*, on top floor World Trade Center.
HOLLAND, MI	Took my son Mike and brother Jim to Lake Michigan for a week.
HOLLAND MI	Tragedy strikes! My brother Jim drowns in rip-tide in Lake Michigan.
HOLLAND, MI	Point West Resort. S2 Yachts awards me 2nd in Nation S2 Yacht Sales

GREEN BAY, WI	Took my son Mike to Carver Yacht Factory, lots of polish sausage.
NORTH HERO, VT	Beautiful Pat Penoyer 25 years younger becomes my 4th wife.
NORTH HERO, VT	Shortly thereafter 2nd wife dies. My soul hurt. Far too tragic.
NORTH HERO, VT	Pat understands that I can't do funeral I'd rather remember her alive.
MONTGOMERY, VT	Ski with kids all day at Jay Peak, dinner at *Zack's on the Rocks*.

1981
REGANOMICS

NORTH HERO, VT	Handwriting is on the wall. This could be my last year in Yacht sales.
NORTH HERO, VT	Interest rates as high as 22%. No one can any longer afford a yacht.
HOLLAND, MI	S2 Yacht Factory feeling the pinch. Sailed Lake Michigan again
MONTREAL, CANADA	Stayed at Chateaux Champlain for two weeks. Probably our last year.
MONTREAL, CANADA	Pat and I did all our favorite Restaurants, *Le St. Amable, La Castellion.*
MONTREAL, CANADA	*La Rhonde, La Maree, La Fille du Roy, Les Halles, La Vert Gallant* etc.
MONTREAL, CANADA	*The Follies,* and Sunday Brunch at Chateau Champlain are always fun.

1982
BANKRUPTCY

North Hero, VT	Like Jackie Gleason said. I've been rich and I've been poor!
North Hero, VT	"Bankruptcy is like being in a sailboat with no wind, It's quiet!" JR
North Hero, VT	Joe Segal visits from Montreal, we often sail together.
North Hero, VT	Knowing I am now poor Joe Segal brings goodies and food.
North Hero, VT	Henry Maloney offers me a job with MONY if I get a get a license.
North Hero, VT	Study, study for Insurance License, took test and got job with MONY.
North Hero, VT	Henry tells me that I got the highest mark ever recorded in Vermont.
North Hero, VT	I believed him and qualified 1st year for Million Dollar Round Table..
Burlington, VT	Henry later admitted, there are only 2 marks, F for Fail, P for Pass.
Colchester, VT	Henry's engine quit in a storm, so I sailed it in to applause from shore.
North Hero, VT	Took investor Crawford Gregory in as 50% partner to manage Marina Internationale and Five oaks until Regonomics blows over.
Burlington, VT	Pat and I moved to condo in Burlington not allowing dogs.
Montpelier, VT	Called Governor's wife, asked her help to find family for Murphy.

Duxbury, VT	Gave Murphy to a farm family on dirt road with two little boys.
Duxbury, VT	The Mother said, "You can visit Murphy at any time."
Duxbury, VT	I can't. This is too emotional for me. I hug Murphy, crying. Bye!

1983
FINANCIAL DYNAMICS CORPORATION

BURLINGTON, VT

Realizing I needed my own company I incorporated a new company.

BENNINGTON, VT

Traveled to every town and hamlet in Vermont to recruit agents.

SWANTON, VT

Recruited 120 licensed agents for my new company

QUECHEE, VT

Must see towns are Manchester, Middlebury, Woodstock and more.

TARRYTOWN, NY

Mom & Dad's Fiftieth Anniversary at Patricia Murphy's Weschester.

NEW YORK CITY, NY

Took Patty for physical fitness interview job. Culture shock prevailed.

NEW YORK CITY, NY

Took Patty to top of Empire State Building before flight to Burlington.

NEWPORT, VT

Catholic Church has spectacular view of entire Lake Mephremagog.

COLCHESTER, VT

Inspired Mike to act *Impossible Dream* from *Man of La Mancha*.

COLCHESTER, VT

The girls cried and the boys clapped and Mike got an A.

BURLINGTON, VT

Helped Mike get his first apartment across the street from MONY.

BURLINGTON, VT

Qualified again for Million Dollar Round Table and got plaque.

1964
UNIVERSITY OF SOUTHERN CALIFORNIA

Los Angeles, CA

MONY Scholarship for Financial Planning at USC Campus - Fantastic!

Santa Monica, CA

Discover *Ye Olde Kings Head Inn* with fellow students. British Pub!

Houston, TX

University of Houston for more campus education paid for by MONY.

Atlanta, GA

Coach Pat Riley of LA Lakers gives lecture on teamwork. Snowed in!

Burlington, VT

Patricia Ann Roach graduates from University of Vermont, BA Degree.

Burlington, VT

All New Jersey relatives attend Patty's graduation Ceremony.

1985
AWARD TRIPS TO VANCOUVER, LAKE TAHOE AND SAN FRANCISCO

BRYN MAR, PA	MONY Scholarship Bryn Mar College for continuing education.
VANCOUVER, CANADA	Qualified for MONY Merit Club. All expense vacation for Pat and I.
VANCOUVER, CANADA	Money's featured speaker was Leo Bascaglia, on Love & Hugging.
VANCOUVER, CANADA	Tea House in Stanley Park, stayed in Vancouver Hilton.
LOS ANGELES, CA	Resigned from MONY and became a General Agent for Transamerica.
BURLINGTON, VT	Opened new office on College St for Financial Dynamics Corporation.
LAKE TAHOE, NV	Invited to Big "O" Club by Transamerica. Bill Cosby, speaker.
LAKE TAHOE, NV	Cruise on Lake Tahoe compliments of Transamerica.
SAN FRANCISCO, CA	MDRT Meeting stayed at the Westin St. Francis.
FT. LAUDERDALE, FL	Transamerica invitation to Bonaventure Spa, a golf resort.

SOUTH BEND, IN	MONY Scholarship to Notre Dame University for Financial Planning.
SOUTH BEND, IN	Notre Dame Sports Museum I found a tie with USC for Heinsman.
BURLINGTON, VT	New 1986 Corvette, yellow with dark plexi-glass removable top.
NEWPORT, VT	Touring Vermont towns in new Corvette helps recruiting effort.
DENVER, CO	Enrolled in the College of Financial Planning for continuing Ed.
BENNINGTON, VT	Touring Vermont I found *Poncho's Wreck* to be good Mexican.
QUEBEC CITY, CANADA	I paid for weekend for two at Chateau Frontenac for FDC best agents.
QUEBEC CITY, CANADA	Comp'd the Financial Dynamics producers for dinner at Le Cavour.

MARTINIQUE

SAN JUAN, PR	Embark with Pat on Chandris MV Azur for 7 day 7 island cruise.
TORTOLA, BVI	Took Pat to my favorite island by Bomba Charger from St. Thomas.
MARTINIQUE	Spent day at Club Med than toured Island to see volcano damage.
DOMINICA	Toured Jungle with Lee and Marge Faucett and Pat. Native dancers.
ST. VINCENT	Busy downtown. Did some interesting restaurants.
BEQUUIA	Tiny island off St. Vincent with beachfront restaurants, very nice.
ST. KITTS	Stayed all day at beach at Jack Tar Resort as I had been here before.
SAN JUAN, PR	Del Moro Fort National Monument at entrance to San Juan Harbor.
CALIS, VT	Gave away my daughter in marriage to Sam Davis at church in Calis.
BOLTON, VT	Patty & Sam's wedding reception at Bolton Valley Lodge.

OTTAWA, CANADA	Took my common law wife Pat for tour of Canada' capital City.
OTTAWA, CANADA	Stayed at *Chateaux Laurier* in Canada' capital City.
OTTAWA, CANADA	Parliament light show with many ice skaters on Ottawa River.
OTTAWA, CANADA	Edgar Degas International Art Exhibit. I got in, Pat didn't, so I left.
BURLINGTON, VT	Amicably became single, moved to two br 2 bath lakefront condo.
BURLINGTON, VT	Pat and I will always feel good about each other but our time was up.
DAYTONA, FL	*Daytona Dog Track*, Mike took his Dad for his first time.
ORLANDO, FL	Mike took his Dad to *Epcott Center* for a great day.
ATLANTA, GA	Transamerica event, snowed in, stayed at Atlanta Marquis Hotel.
CHICAGO, IL	Attended IAFP Convention for week, enjoyed Michigan Ave.
KEENE, NH	Visited newlyweds Patty & Sam. Dinner at *Henry David's*.
ESSEX JUNCTION, VT	John Williams conducts Boston Esplanade Orchestra at Fairgrounds.
ATLANTIC CITY, NJ	Comp'd my parents at *Golden Nugget* for the weekend.

LA JOLLA, CA	Played golf with Henry Maloney at Torre Pines Golf Course.
DAYTONA BEACH, FL	Spent a week at Mike's and did all the hot spots. Big breakfasts.
BOSTON, MA	Visit Pat & Sam's new apartment and did Pubs at Harvard Square.
BURLINGTON, VT	Had season pass to Vermont Mozart Festival.
FT. LAUDERDALE, FL	Second weeks vacation at *Bonaventure Spa,* paid by Transamerica.
CHATHAM, MA	Took Pat and Sam and agents to *Chatham Bars Inn* for get-a-way.
HOUSTON, TX	Dinner at *Charlie's 517.* stayed in elegant hotel by Symphony Hall.

1989
FATHER & SON CROSS COUNTRY ADVENTURE

DAYTONA BEACH, FL   Visited Mike and stayed with him for a
                           few days.

DAYTONA, FL   Mike took his Dad to his first Jai Lai
                           games in Daytona.

BURLINGTON, VT   I got an A in Classical Music course at
                           University of Vermont.

BURLINGTON, VT   After 20 years of no opera, *La Traviatra*
                           in 1st row and I am hooked.

SAN FRANCISCO, CA   Sent Mike R/T tickets to West Coast
                           offering to drive him down coast.

SAN FRANCISCO, CA   Mike saw, *Fisherman's Wharf,* Cable Cars,
                           Transamerica, Chinatown.

SAN FRANCISCO, CA   Rented Lincoln for coastal trip from San
                           Francisco to Tijuana, Mexico.

MONTEREY, CA   *Sly McFly's* Pub in the town John
                           Steinbeck's made famous.

BIG SUR, CA   Spectacular views of the Pacific Coast.

SANTA MONICA, CA   Fish & Ships & Beer at *Ye Ole Kings Head
                           Inn,* walked the park at cliffs.

LOS ANGELES, CA   La Brea Tar Pits, Universal Studio's,
                           Dinner atop Transamerica Tower.

SAN DIEGO, CA   Downtown and Old Town for big beers
                           at O'Hungry's & Mexican food.

TIJUANA, MEXICO   Visit Caesar's Hotel where Caesar Salad
                           was invented. Coronas

LA JOLLA, CA   Mike secures job at La Jolla Taco Bell.
                           Agrees on move to La Jolla.

LA JOLLA, CA	Mike finds room mate to rent house on Fay Ave in La Village.
JACKSONVILLE, FL	Mike meets his Dad at airport in tiny Pontiac for cross country drive.
NEW ORLEANS, LA	First night spent on Bourbon Street. Drag racing on market.
SAN ANTONIO, TX	Alamo closed at 5. Did *Riverwalk,* dinner atop *Tower of America's.*
CARLSBAD, NM	Carlsbad Caverns National Park was an interesting visit.
TUCSON, AZ	Saguaro National Park was impressive. We got here early, in 4 days!
PAGE, AZ	We have extra time, so we headed north for the Grand Canyon.
GRAND CANYON NP,	Father & son do what boys do off the edge of a deep canyon.
ZION NAT. PARK, UT	Very beautiful National Park.
LAS VEGAS, NV	Stopped at Golden Nugget but continued on to California.
PALM SPRINGS, CA	Mexican Restaurant with water sprayed on roof to keep us cool.
DEL MAR, CA	Stayed at Wave Crest, my oceanfront 2BR, 2 Bath Time Share.
DEL MAR, CA	Took Mike's new boss out to dinner. He ordered water, we suggested that he not drink it as it comes from the Colorado River at the bottom of the Grand Canyon. Everyone laughed.
LA JOLLA, CA	Mike starts his new job on Monday, I return to Burlington, VT

BURLINGTON, VT	Formal black tie Strauss Waltz Charity Ball at Radisson Ballroom.
MARTHA'S VINEYARD	Took Patty & Sam for a 3 day weekend get-a-way *Harbor-side Inn.*
BURLINGTON, VT	Golf with Henry Maloney at Burlington Country Club.
BURLINGTON, VT	Flynn Theatre to see Martha Graham's Modern Dance.
MONTREAL, CANADA	Le Jardin de Panos. Greek dinner before ballet with Patty & Sam.
MONTREAL, CANADA	Rimsky-Korsakov's Scheherazade, ballet by Diaghilev is awesome.
LAKE GEORGE, NY	Sagamore Resort. Three day weekend for FDC superstar agents.
DEL MAR, CA	Gave Patty airline tickets to spend a week with me at Wave Crest.
DEL MAR, CA	Patty ran the beach every morning, not as far as Black's Beach. Ha!
TIJUANA, MEXICO	Took Patty, she met a Fayette friend from Marble Island back home.
SAN DIEGO, CA	Took Patty and Mike to O'Hungry's in Old Town for yards of beer.
TORONTO, CANADA	Took Mike by Rapido Train to CN Tower, tallest structure in world.
SAN DIEGO, CA	Mike took his Dad to first Chargers game. Chargers lost to Jets
SAN DIEGO, CA	Told Mike I would join him in La Jolla, as soon as possible.

1990
SOUTHERN CARIBBEAN CRUISE

SAN DIEGO, CA	Beach Boy's Concert with Mike at Jack Murphy Stadium.
ATLANTIC CITY, NJ	Comp'd by parents at Atlantis Casino Hotel. Taught strategy.
ATLANTIC CITY, NJ	Broadway play, *Ain't Misbehaven*, enjoyed Boardwalk.
SAN JUAN, PR	Disembark for Martinique et al on Chandris, SS Americanis.
MARTINIQUE	Beautiful Island, French food everywhere. Did entire island.
ST. LUCIA	Le Toc Resort atop a mountain in Castries to view entire island.
GUADELOUPE	French islands always fascinate me.
ST. JOHN VI	Caneel Bay Plantation where I have often visited and never regret.
ST. MARTIN	Island divided between Dutch and French. Stayed Dutch this time.
BARBADOS	Harrison Cave, the worlds longest was my goal on this visit.
UNION CITY, NJ	My Aunt Marian passed away. Marian J. Roach 1907-1990.
COOPERSTOWN, NY	My first visit to the baseball Hall of Fame, a must experience.
LA JOLLA, CA	Moved from Burlington VT to La Jolla, CA to join my son.
BURLINGTON, VT	Deborah Johnson enters my life 11/18

1990
YEAR OF THE MOVE FROM LAKEFRONT TO OCEANFRONT.

BURLINGTON, VT	La Boheme, Debbie, Patty and Sam to their first opera.
DEL MAR, CA	Debbie's first trip to California, stayed at Wave Crest.
CORONADO, CA	Brunch at Hotel del Coronado.
BURLINGTON, VT	Finished portrait of Debbie.
COOPERSTOWN, NY	Baseball Hall of Fame.
MONTREAL, CANADA	The Follies in Montreal with dinner at Le St. Amable.
SAN DIEGO, CA	Beach Boy's Concert at Jack Murphy Stadium.
BURLINGTON, VT	La Traviata, front row seats to New York City Opera.
MONTREAL, CANADA	Scheherazade ballet, at Place des Art.
VT MOZART FESTIVAL	Outdoor concerts of Vermont Symphony Orchestra often.
LA JOLLA, CA	Debbie's second visit to California at my son's home.
MONTREAL, CANADA	Expos headed for World Series, strike ends the season.
QUEBEC CITY, CANADA	Chateau Frontenac, the Citadel, French Restaurants.
LA JOLLA, CA	Day after Christmas, Debbie joins me forever.

AUTO TOUR OF PACIFIC NORTHWEST AND SOUTHWEST

VICTORIA, BC CANADA	High Tea at the Empress Hotel.
VICTORIA, BC CANADA	Bouchard Gardens visit. How to cover a strip mine.
VANCOUVER, BC CANADA	We drove the entire west coast to Tijuana, Mexico
OLYMPIC NATIONAL PARK	Washington State. Photos of Debbie the model.
SEATTLE, WA	Dinner atop the Space Needle.
PORTLAND, OR	Enjoyed our tour of Portland by trolley.
GLENDENEN BEACH OR	Salishan Lodge for three days of relaxing.
REDWOOD NAT. PARK, CA	Drive thru Redwood Tree. Great stands of Redwoods.
OREGON COASTLINE	Driving the entire west coast to La Jolla, CA
PIPE ORGAN NAT. MON.	Speed trap, got ticket. Lots of pipe organ cactus.
SAGUARO NAT, MON. AZ	Now Saguaro National Park, quite stunning.
SCOTTSDALE, AZ	We stayed at Safari Resort and enjoyed Scottsdale.
PHOENIX, AZ	Felsen House, German restaurant a highlight.
MONTEZUMA CASTLE	National Mon. AZ. Five story Pueblo Village.
CASA GRANDE RUINS, AZ	Pueblo
MONUMENT VALLEY, UT	First visit, no camera, breathtaking beauty at sunset.

Tucson, AZ	Desert Museum, a very good one, learned a lot.
Grand Canyon NP, AZ	Debbie's first visit, my second. Awesome!
Denver, CO	Museum of Natural History, Dinosaur was highlight.
Denver Museum of Art.	Linda, 1983 sculpture is our favorite modern sculpture.
Golden, CO	Coors factory tour.
Ft. Collins, CO	Budweiser factory tour.
Rock Mountain NP	Saw lots of mountain goats.
Cheyenne, WY	Poor Richard's Steak House was a delight.
Laramie, WY	Historic town with good restaurants.
Denver, CO	Brown Palace for Sunday Brunch. Marlow's also fun.
Colorado Springs, CO	US Air Force Academy visit. Chapel is highlight.
Colorado Springs, CO	Broadmore Hotel and Bumble Bee Pub are worth a visit.
Central City, CO	Teller House with the "Face on the Bar Room Floor".
Zion National Park, UT	At Zion you look up, at Bryce you look down.
Bryce Canyon NP, UT	Nature can be wondrous, this park shows it off.
Lake Mead N Rec. NV	Boulder Dam is highlight, massive!
Las Vegas, NV	First overnight at Excalibur Hotel. Debbie loved Vegas.

CORONADO, CA	USS Midway Aircraft Carrier tour, while in service.
TIJUANA, MEXICO	Bullfights, Hemingway taught us of the pageantry.
PASADENA, CA	Santa Anita Racetrack, a premier horseracing venue.
SAN DIEGO, CA	Man of La Mancha, musical at Civic Theatre. Great!
LAS VEGAS, NV	My parents comp'd us at the Sands Resort.
SAN DIEGO, CA	Frank Sinatra live, concert at Sports Arena.
SAN DIEGO, CA	Grand Prix of San Diego. Our first Grand Prix.
TEMECULA, CA	Toured the Wineries of Temecula Valley.

MOVED FROM OCEAN FRONT LA
JOLLA TO MOUNTAIN TOP

La Jolla, CA	Now with a 4 bedroom home we had many guests.
San Diego, CA	Luciano Pavarotti Live Concert. Bravo!
Burlington, VT	Emily Roach Davis born. Now we have a granddaughter.
San Diego, CA	We attended our first baseball All-Star Game.
San Diego, CA	Americus Cup off Point Loma, Dennis Conner wins.
San Francisco	Stayed a week, dined at Empress of China, Kuleto's etc.
Las Vegas, NV	Comp'd by our pal Duncan at Frontier Resort.
San Diego, CA	Symphony Hall, Offenbach, Brahms, Gershwin.
Atlantic City, NJ	Comp'd by my parents at Playboy Resort on boardwalk.
San Diego, CA	Sea World opened our eye's to Jonah and the whale story.
San Diego, CA	Broadway play, "Hair" at Starlight Theatre.
San Francisco	Lots of funny stories dining atop Fairmount Hotel.

DEBBIE AND JOHN'S FIRST CRUISE TOGETHER

LOS ANGELES, CA	Embark on Cunard Sagafjord for 15 day Panama Canal Cruise.
CABO SAN LUCAS	Lands End at the tip of the Baja, Mexico our fist port of call.
ACAPULCO, MEX.	Saw the cliff divers, visited Las Bresas Resort, at flying fish.
COSTA RICA	Spent time at Resort on Puntarenas, saw soccer game.
PANAMA CANAL	Some call it the 9th Wonder of the World, we agree!
ARUBA, NA	Spent day on beach at Aruba Hyatt. Did casino as well.
BARBADOS	Barbados Hilton
FT. LAUDERDALE	Embark again on Cunard Sagafjord for 15 day cruise to Brazil.
EQUATOR	Crossing equator Neptune ceremony aboard Cunard Sagafjord.
EQUATOR	First trip to the South Atlantic Ocean
FRENCH GUIANA	Devils Island French prison of film Papillion and Dryfuss fame.
FORTALEZA, BRAZIL	Fine beaches, beautiful city, historic Old Town.
VITORIA, BRAZIL	Like Curacao, where ship comes down main street to market.
RECIFE, BRAZIL	Cocktails with Dean and Harry Race at Beach Café.

RIO DE JANEIRO	Brazil's finest city. We stayed at the Sheraton Rio.
RIO, BRAZIL	Copacabana Beach a delight.
IPAMINA, BRAZIL	Ipamina Beach, Rio de Janerio is where the action is.
PALM BEACH, FL	Tabu's for lunch, Charlie's for dinner.
ATLANTIC CITY, NJ	Comp'd by my parents to Trump Castle. Good time.
CATALINA, CA	Catalina Island reminds us of Cape Cod, quaint, picturesque.
SAN DIEGO OPERA	Bizet's Carmen.
SAN DIEGO OPERA	Puccini's Madama Butterfly
SAN DIEGO OPERA	Mozart's Don Giovanni

FRENCH POLYNESIA

SOUTH PACIFIC OCEAN	Eventually we hope to sail every ocean on the planet.
BORA BORA,	Michener's Book Hawaii opens with life in Bora Bora.
BORA BORA	Lagoon, Mt. Otemanu, No hustle, just relax in paradise.
TAHITI	Le Royal Tahitian Resort, unusual black sand beach.
TAHITI	Paul Gauguin Museum was worth a visit.
RAIATEA	Stayed a week in a romantic over the water bungalow.
VAHINE ISLAND RESORT	The resort in Raiatea with distant views of Bora Bora.
HUAHINE	Stayed in a hut on the beach.
MOOREA	Enjoyed this island while staying Sofitel La Ora.
LONG BEACH, CA	Cunard Queen Mary, now a hotel. Debbie loved it.
SANTA BARBARA, CA	Stayed with Harry and Dean Race from Brazil cruise.
ATLANTIC CITY, NJ	My parents comp'd Debbie and I at Taj Mahal Resort.
MIDDLEBURY, VT	Stayed in a B&B for Debbie's brother Jerry's wedding.
LOS ANGELES, CA	La Brea Tar Pits, evidence of cataclysmic events.

LOS ANGELES, CA	Dinner atop Transamerica Tower.
SAN FRANCISCO, CA	NFL Playoff Game. NY Giants vs. 49ers. LT retires.
POINT PLEASANT, NJ	Visit Mom and Dad and dine at Lobster Shanty.

FLORIDA LIVING

BOYNTON BEACH. FL	Stayed 3 months to experience Florida living.
BOYNTON BEACH, FL	Discovered "Two Georges" our favorite hangout.
KEY WEST, FL	Took Mom and Debbie to Hemingway Home.
BOCA RATON, FL	Pete Rose's Sports Bar. Pete holds many records.
MIAMI LAKES, FL	We took Mom to Don Shula's, she loved it.
HOMESTEAD, FL	Everglades National Park
NAPLES, FL	Visited my sister.
BILOXI, MS	Took junket from Florida to Biloxi.
BILOXI, MS	Biloxi's beautiful wide beaches like Atlantic city.
GULFPORT, MS	Holiday Inn Beachfront to visit casinos.
NEW ORLEANS, LA	Antoine's & Absinthe on Bourbon Street, Degas B&B.
ANAHEIM, CA	Angels vs. Yankees at Anaheim Stadium.

1996
SOUTH ATLANTIC STATES

FORT SUMTER NAT. MON.   First shots of Civil War.

CHARLESTON, SC   Toured Ft. Sumter, dined Mistral French
                        Restaurant.

HILTON HEAD, SC   From Hyatt Regency, best French is at
                        Café at Wexford.

FREEPORT, BAHAMAS   Biloxi and Atlantic City have impacted
                        Princess Resort.

AMELIA ISLAND, FL   Ritz Carlton nice but Island is for golfers.

DAYTONA BEACH, FL   Enjoyed Winston Cup trials at Daytona
                        Speedway.

ORLANDO, FL   Great Spanish restaurant, Café Tu
                        Tango.

SEBRING, FL   Grand Prix trials on this world class
                        formula 1 circuit.

PAHOKE, FL   Circled Lake Okeechobee. Dinner at
                        Pahokee Marina.

SAN DIEGO, CA   Handel's Messiah at Nazarene College.
                        Terrific!

SD MUSEUM OF ART   Andrew Wyeth "Helga Exhibition" was
                        marvelous.

SAN DIEGO, CA   Rimsky-Korsakov's Malada Procession
                        concert.

YEAR OF PERFORMING ARTS

LOS ANGELES, CA	Valery Gergiev conducts, Berlioz, Romeo & Juliet.
ESCONDIDO, CA	Tchaikovsky's ballet Swan Lake. CA Ballet Co.
TIJUANA, MEXICO	Barber's, Adagio for Strings, Mozart's Violin Concerto #1.
LAGUNA BEACH	Pageant of the Masters at the Festival of the Arts. Must see!
LOS ANGELES, CA	Rattle conducts Beethoven's Ninth at Hollywood Bowl.
SAN DIEGO, CA	Fay Dunaway plays Maria Callas in Master Class. Inspiring.
SAN DIEGO OPERA	Puccini's Turando.
SAN DIEGO OPERA	Verdi's La Traviata
SAN DIEGO OPERA	Gounod's, Romeo & Juliet.
LOS ANGELES, CA	Esa-Pekka Solenen conducts Copland's Salon de Mexico.
SAN DIEGO, CA	First book published, Experience America's Finest City.
CORONADO, CA	USS Kitty Hawk, aircraft carrier tour.
SAN DIEGO, CA	Mainly Mozart Festival at historic Spreckel's Theatre.
DEATH VALLEY	Death Valley National Park,. Lowest spot in the US,
LAS VEGAS, NV	Celebrated birthday at Stephano's, Golden Nugget Resort.

SAN DIEGO, CA	Inaugural Party of Celebrity's new Galaxy Cruise Ship
SAN DIEGO, CA	Moved to 33 floor 2 BR condo at Harbor Club, San Diego.
SAN DIEGO, CA	Tour Nuclear Submarine "La Jolla" at Point Loma. Intense.

1998
IDAHO AND MONTANA

Jackpot, NV	Border town with Idaho, Stayed overnight at Jackpot Casino.
Sun Valley, ID	Ernest Hemingway's last days were spent here.
Salmon, ID	Followed Salmon River from where it starts to Salmon ID.
Eureka, MT	Stayed a week at pal Duncan's Ranch for thanksgiving.
Opera Pacific	Richard Wagner's "Flying Dutchman" so emotional, idealistic.
Opera Pacific	Leoncavallo's "Pagliacci" and Orff's "Carmina Burana." Wow!
San Diego, CA	Burt Bachrach in "What the World Needs Now." We liked it.
San Diego Ballet	Ravel's Bolero, Stravinsky's Rubies at Lyceum Theatre.
San Diego Ballet	Gershwin's Rhapsody in Blue.
San Diego, CA	We attended our first World Series, Padres lost to Yankees.
San Diego, CA	33rd floor of Harbor Club, most awesome residence to date.

LIVING AT HARBOR CLUB AND ENTERTAINING

SAN DIEGO, CA	Entertaining guests all year with spectacular views.
GLEN ROCK, NJ	My home town for St. Like's High 50th class Reunion
GLEN ROCK, NJ	Always good to be back to dine at the Glen Rock Inn.
MET OPERA, NY	Tchaikovsky's "Queen of Spades" Placido Domingo.
NEW YORK CITY	Lincoln Centre, home of Met Opera & NY Philharmonic.
NEW YORK CITY	Lindsay gave us her east side apartment for a weekend.
BOYNTON BEACH, FL	Visiting parents & Two Georges on the inland waterway.
POMPANO BEACH, FL	Seafood Festival's great food. Visited Debbie's brother.
NAPLES, FL	Dinner, Naples Heritage Golf club with parents & sister.
ST PETERSBURG, FL	Dali Museum, quite nice. Lots of Salvatore Dali art.
SAN DIEGO, CA	Spent most of year entertaining guests at Harbor Club.

A YEAR OF STUDY FOR SCREENWRITING

Los Angeles, CA	Took Screenwriting Classes on campus at UCLA
Los Angeles, CA	UCLA at age 64, must still be young at heart.
San Diego, CA	Completed first screenplay, "Mt. Soledad Love Story".
San Diego Opera	Richard Wagner's "Lohengrin" arrives with a swan.
Hollywood, CA	Attended Hollywood Film Festival at Roosevelt Hotel.
San Diego, CA	Completed screenplay, "The Swan" about Wagner.
San Diego, CA	Completed screenplay "Serial Monogamy".
San Diego, CA	Completed Screenplay "Degas"
Santa Monica, CA	Attended a few "Let's Do Lunch" producer meetings.
San Diego, CA	Tour of Giant Tuna Boats with Al Medina. Interesting.
Lakeside, CA	Chartered a bus to take group to Barona Casino often.
Los Angeles, CA	First visit to Getty Museum, masterpiece in architecture.
San Diego Opera	Verdi's "Il Travatore"
San Diego, CA	Grand Prix of San Diego. Our second Grand Prix.
San Diego, CA	Leonard Bernstein's, "Candide"
Coronado, CA	Speed Festival, Sports car racing like the old days.

THE OZARKS AND DEEP SOUTH

BISCAYNE NAT PARK, FL	Took Debbie's brother and his wife.
HOMESTEAD, FL	Everglades, National Park.
BILOXI, MS	Jefferson Davis home Beauvoir on the Gulf of Mexico.
NEW ORLEANS, LA	Edgar Degas Home is today a B&B and worth a visit.
NEW ORLEANS, LA	Jean Lafitte National Park. War of 1812 Chalmette.
NATCHEZ, MS	Natchez Historical Park. Antebellum mansions.
FLINT RIDGE, OK	Stayed a week at Duncan's new home in Oklahoma.
HOT SPRINGS. AR	Hot Springs National Park where FDR sought cure.
EUREKA HOT SPRINGS, AR	A destination during the great days of the railroad
OZARK NATIONAL FOREST	Ozark mountain range is very beautiful.
PEA RIDGE NATIONAL PARK	Civil War battle took place at Pea Ridge, Arkansas.
GROVE, OK	Lake O'Cherokees and Har-ber Village worth a visit.
FLINT RIDGE, OK	Pal Duncan treats us again to an Oklahoma Barbecue.
TULSA, OK	Tour of the city for Debbie and I.
MEMPHIS, TN	Beal Street, the Rum Boogie café and the Piedmont.
MEMPHIS, TN	Graceland. The Elvis Presley home, now a museum.

THREE STATES REMAIN *, TO SEE ALL FIFTY

SONOMA, CA — Visited and photographed all 21 California Missions for book.

CARMEL. CA — Visited Padre Junipero Serra's grave at Carmel Mission.

SALINAS, CA — John Steinbeck's home. I have read all his books.

LAKE TAHOE, NV — Relax at Harrah's after visiting all 21 California Missions.

WYOMING — Grand Teton National Park.

WYOMING — Yellowstone National Park. Timed it just right for old faithful.

MONTANA — Big Horn National Forest. Too beautiful.

MONTANA — Custer National Monument. Arrived at dusk, visualize battle.

NORTH DAKOTA * — Theodore Roosevelt National Park. Created Nat. Park System.

SOUTH DAKOTA * — Mount Rushmore National Monument, Impressive close up.

DEADWOOD, SD — 81 casinos including Cadillac Jack's where we lost few bucks.

SOUTH DAKOTA — Wind Cave National Park, herds of buffalo roaming.

SOUTH DAKOTA — Jewel Cave National Monument

NEBRASKA * — Nebraska completes my visit to all 50 states.

NEBRASKA — Agate Fossil Beds National Monument.

NEBRASKA	Scott's Bluff national Monument.
TAOS, NM	Taos Pueblo since 1680 revolt, a World Heritage Site.
TAOS, NM	Kit Carson's home.
ARIZONA	Petrified Forest National Park and the Painted Desert.
SEDONA, AZ	Quite beautiful, the red rocks, Holy Cross Chapel and vortex.
CALIFORNIA	Joshua Tree National Park, our 3rd visit, a favorite.
CALIFORNIA	Anza-Borrego State Park. Largest in US. Font's Point a must.

BURLINGTON, VT	Combine family visits with photos for Vermont Book.
BURLINGTON, VT	Ethan Allen Homestead and grave site photos taken.
TICONDEROGA, NY	The Gibraltar like Fortress of the Revolutionary War
SARATOGA, NY	Saratoga Battlefield National Park, turning point of war..
SARATOGA, NY	Benedict Arnold led the charge defeating British.
ORWELL, VT	Mt. Independence. Climbed to top.
HUBBARDTON, VT	Seth Warner held off British in read guard battle.
SUNDERLAND, VT	Ira Allen's home is now a Bed & Breakfast.
BENNINGTON, VT	Fay's Catamount Tavern made famous by Ethan Allen.
BENNINGTON, VT	Bennington Battle Monument, Vermonter's beat British.
WALMOOSAC, NY	Where the Battle of Bennington took place.
SHOREHAM, VT	Enos home, Ethan Allen and Benedict Arnold argue.
TICONDEROGA, NY	Mt. Defiance. British haul canons up mountain.
SCHUYLERVILLE, NY	Saratoga Battlefield Monument, Burgoyne surrenders.

SKEENSBORO, NY	Birthplace of US Navy. Benedict Arnold built ships.
CROWN POINT, NY	Fort St. Frederick ruins from the French and Indian War.
CROWN POINT, NY	Fort Amhearst redoubts from the Revolutionary War.
TICONDEROGA, NY	Fort Carrillon renamed Fort Ticonderoga.
COLCHESTER, VT	Champagne Brunch on my daughter's new deck.
WINOOSKI, VT	Visit Stella Frenette, my favorite mother in law.
NORTH HERO, VT	Visit Marina Internationale a monument I created.
COLCHESTER, VT	Visit home I designed and built as another monument.
MARACOPA, AZ	Weekend at Harrah's Phoenix Resort.
SHELBURNE, VT	Jen and Michael Cairns wedding at Shelburne Farms.
SAN DIEGO, CA	Invited by CCBA President to Candelas Restaurant.

CANADIAN AND AMERICAN ROCKIES

CALGARY, CANADA	Since 9-11 a Passport to enter Canada is advised.
BANFF, ALBERTA, CANADA	Banff Springs Hotel, built by Canadian Pacific.
LAKE LOUISE, ALBERTA	Chateau Lake Louise another awesome CP Hotel
PROVO, UTAH	Dinosaur National Monument. Don't miss this one.
MONUMENT VALLEY, UT	One of our favorite places on earth. Spectacular!
GRAND CANYON, AZ	El Tavor Lodge for a Sunday Brunch.
JACKSON HOLE, WY	Cowboy Bar, Cadillac Restaurant, Teton Village.
WYOMING	Second visit to Grand Teton National Park
WYOMING	Second visit to Yellowstone National Park
MOAB, UT	Arches National Park. Beautiful and well groomed.
OGDEN UT	Wide streets, Historic district at 25th street.
IDAHO FALLS, ID	Smitty's Steak House get award for best breakfast.
KAYENTA, AZ	Navajo ruins 12691300 Navajo National Monument.
TECATE, MEXICO	Rancho Tecate Ressort for Sunday Brunch.
WHITEFISH, MT	Bulldog's Saloon last visited in 1998
LIVINGSTON, MT	Stayed a week at Duncan's home on Yellowstone River.

LIVINGSTON, MT	Stockman's, O'Ryan's, Chop House, and the Owl.
LAS VEGAS, NV	Comp'd 68 nights at resorts in Las Vegas and Laughlin.
MESQUITE, NV	Border town with Utah. Stayed at Oasis Resort.
VALLEY CENTER, CA	Took Mike & Lori to Sunday Brunch at Harrah's Rincon.
LAS VEGAS, NV	Attained Diamond level at Rio before Thanksgiving.
VALLEY CENTER, CA	Debbie attained Platinum level before Christmas.
SAN DIEGO, CA	Took Mike & Lori to Waterfront and to Crab shack.
LAUGHLIN, NV	Debbie hits $6,000.00 jackpot on 1 dollar at Harrah's.

DESERT RESORTS

SANTA FE, NM	Visit Mike and Lori's new adobe home in Santa Fe.
SANTA FE, NM	Attended Screenwriters Conference 2005 in Santa Fe.
SANTA FE, NM	San Miguel Mission. 1610, oldest church in US.
SANTA FE, NM	The Shed, father's Day celebration by Mike & Lori.
SANTA FE, NM	Marisos La Playa, Took Mike and Lori.
TOMBSTONE, AZ	Wyatt Earp Historic Site, gunfight at OK Corral.
MARACOPA, AZ	Two free nights at Harrah's AK-Chin Resort.
PHOENIX, AZ	Saguaro National Park, 3rd visit so we did east park.
LAS VEGAS, NV	17 days, 5 days at Rio Suites, 12 days in Laughlin.
VALLEY CENTER, CA	Hit a $1,250 jackpot at Harrah's Rincon.
LAS VEGAS, NV	Wynn Resort opens with 2 free nights + 2 at Rio.
LAS VEGAS, NV	Stage Deli at Caesars and Carnegie Deli at Mirage.
SAN DIEGO, CA	Fine dining at Candelas and Mare & Monti

GRAND TOUR OF EUROPE

GALVESTON, TX	Embark on Celebrity, Galaxy for Trans-Atlantic crossing.
PUNTA DELGADA, AZORES	Azores largest city and capital. Very green.
LISBON, PORTUGAL	Lots of Monuments of Portuguese explorers.
FATIMA, PORTUGAL	120 miles north of Lisbon, site of miracle of Fatima.
PALMA DE MALLORCA	Capital of Mallorca, largest of the Ballaric Islands.
PETRA, MALLORCA	Birthplace of Fr. Junipero Serra. Research for book.
ROME, ITALY	Coliseum, Forum, Trivi Fountain, Spanish Steps.
VATICAN CITY, ITALY	St. Peter's, Sistine Chapel
ORVIETO, ITALY	Home base for Rome, Sienna and Etruscan Hill Towns.
CIVITA, ITALY	Etruscan Hill town for a medieval experience. B&B
FLORENCE, ITALY	Art, architecture.
ASSISI, ITALY	St. Francis Basilica atop this Etruscan Hill town.
REUTTE, AUSTRIA	Our home base for Bavaria in the Austrian Tirol region.
FUSSEN, GERMANY	King Ludwig II's romantic Newschwanstein Castle.
MUNICH, GERMANY	Beer Halls, Palace of Bavarian Kings.
BERG, GERMANY	Lake Sternberg, where King Ludwig II died.

SALZBURG, AUSTRIA	Lots of Mozart's music and Mozart's home.
VIENNA, AUSTRIA	Strauss waltz, Danube River Cruise, stayed a week.
BAYREUTH, GERMANY	Wagner's Festspeilhaus and home, spent 4 days here.
STUTTGART, GERMANY	World Cup Soccer sponsored by Germany this year.
STRASBURG, FRANCE	Wine Country
BEAUNNE, FRANCE	Wine Country
COLMAR, FRANCE	Wine Country
AMBOISE, FRANCE	Chateau Amboise
BLOIS, FRANCE	Home base for Chateau Chenonceau and Chambois.
PARIS, FRANCE	Debbie loved Paris.
AVIGNON, FRANCE	Residence of Pope when they moved from Italy.
NICE, FRANCE	We enjoyed Nice so much we stayed 12 days.
PORTO FINO, ITALY	Visited twice, once by car and once by ship.
SANTORINI, GREECE	Buildings built on rim of volcano that the sea has filled.
KUSADASI, TURKEY	"Temple of Artimus" an Ancient Wonder of the World.
EPHESUS, TURKEY	St. Paul preached to the Ephesians. The ancient Library.
YALTA, UKRAINE	Roosevelt, Stalin and Churchill met at Yalta Conference.
SOCHI, RUSSIA	Black Sea Resort used as Russian Camp David.

SEVASTAPOL, UKRAINE	Many war memorials, a pleasant place.
ODESSA, UKRAINE	Mozart Café for lunch. The beautiful Opera House.
CONSTANTA, ROMANIA	People watch along the promenade by Black Sea.
NESBUR, BULGARIA	Old town is a World Heritage Site.
ISTANBUL, TURKEY	Three days to visit the Mosques, Bazaar and city.
RHODES, GREECE	Site of "Colossus of Rhodes" Ancient Wonder of World.
MYKONOS, GREECE	Our favorite Greek Island. Windmills and alleys.
TROY, TURKEY	Marked well on cliff, Homer's city finely discovered.
ATHENS, GREECE	Acropolis, Parthenon, Tavernas in the Placka, wonderful.
PIRAEUS, GREECE	Great dinning overlooking Piraeus harbor.
AMALFI, ITALY	Don't miss the Amalfi Coast of Italy. Quite beautiful.
NAXOS, SICILY	Mt. Etna, the smoking volcano is a backdrop for this city.
KOTOR MONTENEGRO	Southernmost fjord in Europe. A World Heritage Site.
DUBROVNIK, CROATIA	Medieval walled city designated a World Heritage Site.

VENICE, ITALY	Stayed 3 days in Venice, enjoyed the canals and people.
POMPEII, ITALY	Awesome!
CAPRI, ITALY	Funicular to top of island
CORSICA	French Mediterranean Island, Birthplace of Napoleon..
MONACO	The mother of all casinos, Monte Carlo. Elegant!
MARSEILLE, FRANCE	A fun city for malls and outdoor cafes.
BARCELONA, SPAIN	Las Ramblas, Took flight to Copenhagen, Denmark
COPENHAGEN, DENMARK	Embark of HAL ship Amsterdam for Baltic Sea Cruise.
TALLINN, ESTONIA	I have a friend born in Estonia that made it interesting.
ST. PETERSBURG, RUSSIA	Three wonderful days in this beautiful city.
HELSINKI, FINLAND	Architectural marvels: the opera house and Finlandia. Stockholm, Sweden City to award the Nobel Prize, Mt. Soledad Love Story?
VISBY, SWEDEN	Walled city on Gotland Island built in 1200.
BERLIN, GERMANY	Brandenburg Gate, Unter den Linden, Einstein Café.
AARHUS, DENMARK	Established in 940 as Viking settlement.
COPENHAGEN, DENMARK	Tivoli Gardens. We drank our share of Tuborg Beer.

OSLO, NORWAY	Viking Museum has 3 original Viking ships.
KRISTIANSAND, NORWAY	The Southernmost part of Norway, close to Denmark.
BERGEN, NORWAY	Gabled wooden homes, a World Heritage Site.
TORSHAUN, FAROE ISLANDS	Critical islands for St. Brendon's voyage to America.
AKUREYRI, ICELAND	Vikings arrived here in 890.
ISAFJORDUR, ICELAND	These towering fjords are the least visited in Iceland.

REYKJAVIK, ICELAND	Irish monks settled here in 750.
GREENLAND	St. Christian Sound glaciers calving icebergs. Wow! Quaqortoc, Greenland In 972 Eric the Red settled here with 400 -500 settlers.
ST. ANTHONY, CANADA	Lief Ericson, founded first settlement in America in 999.
L'ANSE AU MEDOWS	St. Anthony, Newfoundland, Canada hard evidence 999.
ST. JOHN'S, NF CANADA	Natural harbor, lots of fishing boats, Water Street cafes,
NEW YORK CITY, NY	Statue of Liberty greets us after Grand Tour of Europe.

WORLD CRUISE- FIVE MONTHS

LOS ANGELES, CA	Embark on QE2, Cunard Queen Elizabeth II.
SAN FRANCISCO, CA	First time arriving by ship under Golden Gate.
HONOLULU, HA	Kahula Resort, north of Diamond Head. Nice.
PAPEETE, TAHITI, FP	We visited French Polynesia in 1994, 2nd visit.
MOOREA, FP	South Pacific filmed here. Jagged Mountains.
NUKU'ALOFA, TONGA	Constitutional Monarchy governed by a King.
SUVA, FIJI	If invited for dinner, cannibalism existed until 1920.
AUCKLAND, NEW ZEALAND	City of sails, 70,000 watercraft. One in 4 own boat.
WELLINGTON, NZ	Capital of New Zealand with impressive architecture.
CHRISTCHURCH, NZ	Bought Debbie a bracelet for Valentine's Day.
HOBART, TASMANIA	Australia's most environmental culture, the Tassies.
SYDNEY, AUSTRALIA	Stayed 9 days. Saw Opera "Alcina" Sydney Opera.
SYDNEY, AUSTRALIA	Major celebration with QE2 and QM2 both in port.
BRISBANE, AUSTRALIA	Debbie won at Treasury Casino.

WHITSUNDAY IS. AUSTRALIA	Hamilton Beach Resort for Great Barrier Reef.
CAIRNS, AUSTRALIA	Pronounced kanz, modern tropical city.
DARWIN, AUSTRALIA	Bombed by Japanese in WWII and rebuilt modern.
BALI, INDONESIA	Terraced rice fields, temples, people in harmony.
SEMARANG, INDONESIA	Port city for Java, Indonesia
SINGAPORE	Raffle's Hotel frequented by famous authors.
NHA TRANG, VIET NAM	The White Buddha and the Sleeping Buddha, interesting.
HONG KONG, CHINA	Enjoyed Kowloon and shops on Canton Road.
XIAMEN, CHINA	Nationalist Chinese left Xiamen for Taiwan
SHANGHAI, CHINA	Both Colonial and super modern architecture.
BEIJING, CHINA	Great Wall of China, Forbidden City.
DELIAN, CHINA	Formerly Manchuria with Japanese and Russians.
HONG KONG, CHINA	Our 2nd visit we took a high speed ferry to Macou,
MACAU, CHINA	Formerly a Portuguese Territory, now filled with casinos.
SAIGON, VIETNAM	Now called Ho Chi Minh City. French influence.
BANGKOK, THAILAND	Formerly Siam. Smiling faces of happy people.

SINGAPORE	Our 2nd visit for a Singapore Sling cocktail.
PHUKET, THAILAND	Hot day, most people enjoyed the beaches.
GOA, INDIA	Meera met us at the dock and took us to her home.
MUMBAI (BOMBAY) INDIA	The Gate and the Taj Mahal Hotel all day.

SALALAH, OMAN	Lots of sand, camels, busy refueling port.
LUXOR, EGYPT	Temples of Luxor and tombs from 1540 BC.
LUXOR, EGYPT.	Valley of the Kings, King Tot's Tomb.
AQUABA, JORDAN	Made famous by Lawrence of Arabia.
EILIAT, ISRAEL	Jordan will not allow entry of you go to Eliot.
SUEZ CANAL, EGYPT	Transit Suez Canal from Red Sea to Port Said.
CAIRO, EGYPT.	Pyramids, survive as Ancient Wonder of World.
DELPHI, GREECE	Ancient Delphi excavated & restored by French.
BRUSSELS, BELGIUM	Ripped off by car rental agency.
BRUGES, BELGIUM	Walled city that is very interesting.
AMSTERDAM, NETHERLANDS	Too rainy for canal trip. Lunch by Opera House.
LUXEMBURG	Grand Cravat Hotel was our base with great views.
LIECHTENSTEIN	Dinner overlooking the castle of the Prince .
MOSELLE VALLEY, GERMANY	Followed the Mosell River until it meets the Rhine
BACHRACH, GERMANY	So many castles on a Rhine River Cruise,
ROTHERSBERG, GERMANY	A medieval walled town on the Romantic Road.

NICE, FRANCE	Stayed 9 more days, same hotel last years 12 days.
MONACO	Embarked on Holland America's Rotterdam VI.
MARSEILLE, FRANCE	Always a pleasure doing the outdoor café's.
BARCELONA, SPAIN	All day enjoying Tapas on Las Ramblas.
CADIZ, SPAIN	Walled city on Atlantic coast with Roman ruins.
LISBON, PORTUGAL	Enjoyed the city and its history.
PARIS, FRANCE	Saine River Cruise on Bateau Moushe. Awesome!
LONDON, ENGLAND	From Harwich to Heathrow for flight to Ireland.
CORK, IRELAND	Roach family immigrated from Cork Ireland.
BLARNEY, IRELAND	Yes, I kissed the Blarney stone twice 1 for Debbie.
DINGLE, IRELAND	So many Irish Pubs. Gallic still spoken in Dingle.
DUBLIN, IRELAND	Guinness Factory postponed. Too much rain.
LONDON, ENGLAND	Return to Heathrow for trip to Southampton.
SOUTHAMPTON ENGLAND	Embark on Cunard Queen Mary II Transatlantic.
NEW YORK CITY	Statue of Liberty greets us just like last year.
BURLINGTON, VT	Took granddaughter Sweetwater's & Tortilla Flat.
LAS VEGAS, NV	Ten Days at Rio and Paris, won $800.00

SOUTH AMERICA AND ANTARCTICA CRUISE

FT. LAUDERDALE, FL	Embark on Holland America's Princendam.
CAYMAN ISLANDS	Still re-building after hurricane.
COSTA RICA	Puerto Limon is Atlantic port, we have done Pacific port.
PANAMA CANAL	Our 2nd transit, this time fro Atlantic to Pacific.
PANAMA CITY, PANAMA	30,000 Americans live here. Many modern high-rises.
MANTA, ECUADOR	Panama hat was invented here & today is big business.
GUAYAQUIL, ECUADOR	Spanish invasion caused Gay to murder his wife Quil.
TRUJILLO, PERU	The port Salaverry serves Trujillo AND Machu Pichu.
LIMA, PERU	Spent two days in the Miraflores area of Lima. Nice.
ARICA, CHILE	Pre-fab cathedral designed by Eiffel in France.
COQUIMBO, CHILE	Chile's wine country is world famous.
SANTIAGO, CHILE	Valparaiso, Santiago's seaport is a World Heritage Site.
PUERTO MOTT, CHILE	German population for sausage, sauerbraten and beer.
PUERTO CHACABUCCO CHILE	Wild fires and tsunami destroyed original Puerto Aisen.
PUNTA ARENAS, CHILE	Patagonia, 3rd largest city in Patagonian region.

TERRA DEL FUEGO	High snow capped mountains in Chile and Argentina.
USHUAIA, ARGENTINA	Southernmost city in the world. Airport to Antarctica.
ANTARCTICA	Drake Passage was roughest day at sea. 18 ft waves.
WILHELM ARCHIPELAGO	Antarctica research stations of Chile, UK, Argentina.
ANVERS IS. ANTARCTICA	US Palmer Station Research Center, 40 scientists.
ELEPHANT IS. ANTARCTICA	22 marooned men saved by Shaklelton's bravery.
SOUTH GEORGIA	British territory and grave site of Shakelton.
FALKLAND ISLANDS	Iron Lady Margaret Thatcher went to war Argentina.
BUENOS AIRES, ARGENTINA	Couples Tango on the sidewalks, very romantic city.
BUENOS AIRES, ARGENTINA	Replaced Debbie's stolen bracelet at H. Stern's.
MONTEVIDEO, URUGUAY	Haircuts for booth of us. Dined in outdoor cafes.
MONTEVIDEO, URUGUAY	Nazi ship scuttled in harbor. Mast above water.
RIO DE JANERIO, BRAZIL	Two days at Ipamina Beach, Lots of Brazilian beer.
RIO DE JANERIO, BRAZIL	H Stearn's again to upgrade Debbie's tennis bracelet.
SALVADOR, BRAZIL	High on a hill with a beautiful town square.

RECIFE, BRAZIL	Had a great time in Recife in 1993 as well.
FORTALEZA, BRAZIL	Always fun walking along the beachfront hotels.
AMAZON RIVER CRUISE	The Princendam enters Amazon River bound for Manaus.
BELEM. BRAZIL	First port on Amazon River. An adventure awaits us.

SANTARUM, BRAZIL	The Rio Tapajco, joins the Amazon. Piranhas fish.
BOCA DE VALARIA, BRAZIL	Jungle native village. Natives greet you in canoes.
AMAZON RIVER, BRAZIL	Deforestation taking place causing global warming.
MANAUS, BRAZIL	Manaus, where Rio Negro & Rio Solimoes join Amazon.
MANAUS, BRAZIL	Taetro Amazonas Opera House 1000 miles from cities.
MANAUS, BRAZIL	European Rubber Barons built the Taetro Amazonas.
MANAUS, BRAZIL	Attended concert by Amazonas Philharmonic.
PARINTINS, BRAZIL	High curbs, slippery sidewalks.
FRENCH GUIANA	Second visit since 1993, beautiful island.
BARBADOS	Ships must like this port, visited 1993, 1990, 2008, 2010.
MAYAQUEZ, PUERTO RICO	Mayor went all out to attract cruise ships. Great party.
FT. LAUDERDALE, FL	Circled South America now fly back to San Diego.

2009
SEA OF CORTEZ CRUISE

SAN DIEGO, CA	Embark Holland America's Volendam to Sea of Cortez.
LORETO, MEXICO	Mission Loreto photo op for book on California.
MAZATLAN, MEXICO	Nice beaches, 2nd largest city on Mexico's pacific coast.
TOPOLOBAMBO, MEXICO	Shrimp boats galore. Los Mochis is 25 miles inland.
LOS MOCHIS, MEXICO	Great restaurants serving seafood. Spent the day here.
CABO SAN LUCAS, MEXICO	Our second visit. Many new condos shows big growth.
LAUGHLIN, NV	Thanksgiving weekend at the Golden Nugget Resort.
ESCONDIDO, CA	Reenactment of the Battle of San Pasquale on Dec.6.
LAS VEGAS, NV	Phantom of the Opera, Broadway Play at the Venetian.
SAN DIEGO OPERA	Verdi's "Nubucco", Nebuchadnezzar, King of Babylon.

ALASKA CRUISE

SAN DIEGO, CA	Embark of HAL Rotterdam VI for Vancouver, Canada.
VICTORIA, BC CANADA	Met Cecile Corcoran Claus & Joyce Ligon.
VANCOUVER, BC CANADA	Embark of Celebrity Millennium for Alaska Cruise.
KETCHIKAN, ALASKA	Small Alaskan fishing village gets you in Alaskan spirit.
ICY STRAIGHT PT. ALASKA	We would rather visit Sitka, this is an Indian reservation.
JUNEAU, ALASKA	Capital of Alaska. No roads in or out. Lots of Saloons.
SKAGWAY, ALASKA	The Red Onion Saloon, so authentic from Klondike days.
HUBBARD GLACIER	Ship came up real close to see glacier calving.
SEWARD, ALASKA	Took Grandview Train 4 hrs to Anchorage. Spectacular!
ANCHORAGE, ALASKA	Stayed overnight in Anchorage for flight to San Diego.
LAS VEGAS, NV	Venetian Resort has become our favorite with Paris.
SAN FRANCISCO, CA	Three day trip for photos for Book on California.
JENNER, CA	Fort Ross the Russian settlement in California.
BODEGA BAY, CA	Spectacular scenery, like the Big Sur.

SONOMA, CA	Wine country, Bear Flag Memorial here also.
SONOMA, CA	General Mariano Guadeloupe Vallejo's home. A Patriot.
COLOMA, CA	Gold discovered at Sutter's Mill, causing gold rush.
SACRAMENTO, CA	Sutter's Fort, a way station for settlers to California.
SACRAMENTO, CA	CA State Railroad Museum has one of 2 Golden Spikes.
LOS ANGELES OPERA	Wagner's Ring Cycle takes a week. Stay at Omni Hotel.
SANTA MONICA, CA	Ye Old Kings Head Inn for Fish and Chips.
LOS ANGELES OPERA	Das Rheingold, 1st opera of Wagner's Ring Cycle
LOS ANGELES OPERA	Die Walkure, 2nd opera of Wagner's Ring Cycle.
LOS ANGELES OPERA	Siegfried, 3rd opera of Wagner's Ring Cycle
LOS ANGELES OPERA	Gotterdammerung, 4th and last of Wagner's Ring Cycle.
SAN DIEGO, CA	Our wonderful 21 year marriage ends as God takes Debbie, from me on Nov.4 2010.

START SECOND WORLD CRUISE

SAN DIEGO, CA	Encouraged by friends to continue lifestyle without Debbie.
MIAMI, FL	Embark Costa Atlantica for Trans-Atlantic Cruise to Europe.
NASSAU, BAHAMAS	Visited Paradise Island Casino and lost a few bucks.
DOMINICAN REPUBLIC	Cruise Line owns Catalina Island, not impressive.
TORTOLA, BVI	Always a favorite. Long Bay Resort still pristine.
ANTIGUA	Walked through town, ended up at bar to people watch.
TENERIFE, CANARY ISLANDS	A most beautiful island off the African Coast.
MADEIRA, PORTUGAL	Also a beautiful Island off the African Coast.
MALAGA, SPAIN	Attempted to travel inland to the Alhambra, but failed.
CORFU GREECE	2nd visit, walked through town and enjoyed the people.
DUBROVNIK, CROATIA	Hank and I in tavern across from fountain greeted travelers.
VENICE, ITALY	Arriving by ship is fantastic. Flight to Barcelona, Spain.
MALLORCA	Spent 3 days here, love this island. My second visit.
BARCELONA, SPAIN	Embark on Holland America, Nieuw Amsterdam.

CINC TERRE REGION, ITALY	Five little villages on Italian Riviera. Wonderful!
ROME, ITALY	Last time here, threw coins in Trevi Fountain. Here I am!
MESSINA, SICILY	Big city, not much happening on a Sunday.
NAUPLION, GREECE	Beautiful resort town with lots of European tourists.
DUBROVNIK, CROATIA	4th visit. This time learned of massacre of youth.
VENICE, ITALY	Imagine three wonderful days in this city of canals.
VENICE, ITALY	Dinner at the one and only original Harry's Bar.
VENICE, ITALY	St Mark's Square. There never was a St. Mark!
SPLIT, CROATIA	Very nice, walked through city, many taverns, fun people.
ATHENS (PIRAEUS) GREECE	Bought new pair of Top Siders, Euro driving costs up.
ISTANBUL, TURKEY	Spent 2 more days here for a total of 5 days on earlier trip.
MYKONOS, GREECE	Always a favorite, love this place, inflation out of control.
EPHESUS, TURKEY	Third visit. Spent the day at the Bazaar.
SANTORINI, GREECE	This time walked down volcano on donkey path. Feet hurt.
KATAKOLON, GREECE	Lots of waterfront cafes. Took an hour train ride to Olympia.
OLYMPIA GREECE.	Ancient Wonder of the World, 2nd only to Pyramids of Giza.

VENICE, ITALY	Love arriving by ship. Took flight to Dublin.
DUBLIN, IRELAND	Guinness Factory is a must experience in Ireland.
SAN DIEGO SYMPHONY	Lang Lang plays Tchaikovsky's Piano Concerto # 1.
SAN DIEGO, CA	Prokofiev's Ballet, Cinderella, Russian Ballet Co. Moscow.
LOS ANGELES OPERA	Eugene Onegin, a Peter Tchaikovsky, Opera. Very good.
SAN DIEGO CITY BALLET	Striven ski's Firebird, Shostakovich HCIV-OKAT-SOHS.
SAN DIEGO, OLD GLOBE	August; Osage County. A play full of arguments.
SAN DIEGO SYMPHONY	Four Seasons, by Vivaldi, Glazunov and Glass. All good.
ATLANTA, GA	14 hour flight to Johannesburg, South Africa.
JOHANNESBURG, SO. AFRICA	1st Meeting of 12 Safari members at Westcliff Hotel.
ZIMBABWE, AFRICA	Victoria Falls. A natural Wonder of the World.
ZAMBEZI, AFRICA	Victoria Falls flows to Zambezi River to Indian Ocean.
BOTSWANA, AFRICA	Chobe Chilwero Hotel with separate huts alert for leopards.

BOTSWANA, AFRICA	Safari, herds of elephant, antelope and many lions
BOTSWANA, AFRICA	Safari
NAMIBIA, AFRICA	Photo op for hippopotami on Chobe River.
ZIMBABWE, AFRICA	Forced checking of carry-on luggage. Computer Stolen.
CAPE TOWN, SO. AFRICA	Two days in Cape Town. Bought new notebook computer.
CAPE TOWN, SO. AFRICA	Embark on Oceana Nautica to complete 2nd World Cruise
EAST LONDON, SO. AFRICA	Nelson Mandela's integration working well.
DURBAN, SO. AFRICA	Promenade along beautiful beaches. Cargo Hold Restaurant.
MAPUTO, MOZAMBIQUE	A bustling city with lots of traffic and huge population.
FRENCH COMOROS	Island in the channel between Madagascar and Mozambique

FINISH SECOND WORLD CRUISE

MADAGASCAR, NOSY BE	Small town on New Years Day, very pleasant.
MAURITIUS, PORT LEWIS	English Colony, Top tourist destination in Africa.
REUNION ISLAND	Upscale Parisian shopping at Pointe de Galette.
SEYCHELLES, MAHE	Largest isle 60 beaches with night clubs and casinos.
SEYCHELLES, LA DIGUE	Thought to be Garden of Eden. Laid back island.
SEYCHELLES, PRESLIN	Anse Lazio voted to top ten beaches in the world.
MALDIVES, MALE	200 inhabited islands out of 1190 atolls.
MANGALORE, INDIA	Exports cashew nuts and coffee from Arabian Sea.
COCHIN, INDIA	Visited by tuk tuk the historic fishing nets.
COLOMBO, SRI LANKA	New Opera House cost 3 billion rupees is world class.
GALLE, SRI LANKA	Fort built by Dutch is a World Heritage Site.
TRINCOMALEE, INDIA	One of the finest deep water harbors in the world.
PHUKET, THAILAND	Patong Beach where 50,000 killed in 2004 Tsunami.
PENANG, MALAYSIA	The Pearl of the Orient on the Malay Peninsula.

KUALA LUMPUR, MALAYSIA	Fantastic city, on track to be much like Singapore.
SINGAPORE	Chinese, Malay, Hindu and English living in harmony
AUCKLAND, NEW ZEALAND	Enjoyed 3 days. Embarked on Celebrity Century.
TAURANGA, NEW ZEALAND	Fastest growing city in New Zealand.
AKAOROA, NEW ZEALAND	Quaint town with French influence and big harbor.
DUNEDIN, NEW ZEALAND	19th Century Edwardian and Victorian architecture.
DUSKY SOUND, NEW ZEALAND	The largest fjord discovered by Captain Cook in 1770
DOUBTFUL SOUND, NZ	Doubtful as Capt. Cook feared he could not turn ship.
MILFORD SOUND, NZ	Most beautiful fjord with glaciers calving icebergs.
SYDNEY, AUSTRALIA	Love it!. Spent 11 days here in 2007. Return often.
SYDNEY, AUSTRALIA,	Embark of Celebrity Century to circle Australia.
MELBOURNE, AUSTRALIA	Kangaroos all sleeping in Melbourne Zoo.
ADELAIDE, AUSTRALIA	Rundel Street has 700 retail stores operates as a mall.
ALBANY, AUSTRALIA	In World War I the Australian Fleet anchored here.
BUNBURY, AUSTRALIA	A desirable city with a small town atmosphere.

FREEMANTLE, AUSTRALIA	Pubs and night life in Fremantle are outstanding.
PERTH, AUSTRALIA	Enjoy Murray, Hay and London St and the Bell Tower
GERALDTON, AUSTRALIA	Located 23 miles north of Perth, less than 40,000 pop.
BROOME, AUSTRALIA	Small town atmosphere makes Broome a lot of fun.
BALI, INDONESIA	The beach at Kuta is a pure delight. Beach Bars too.
2012 CONTINUED.	
DARWIN, AUSTRALIA	Bombed 60 times by Japanese.
CAIRNS, AUSTRALIA	A departure City for the Great Barrier Reef.
BRISBANE, AUSTRALIA	Koalas and leaping Kangaroos, by Ian & Monica.
SYDNEY, AUSTRALIA	With so many pubs in the Rocks Area, Try them all.
PAPEETE, TAHITI, FR. POLYNESIA	2nd visit to these islands and it is good to be back.
MOOREA, FRENCH POLYNESIA	Jagged mountains rising from the sea, quite pretty.
BORA BORA, FRENCH POLYNESIA	A paradise!
RAIATEA, FRENCH POLYNESIA	Considerable growth since my last visit.
LAHAINA, HAWAII	On the island of Maui, today a hot spot for tourism.
HONOLULU, HAWAII	Still less than 1 million population on Oahu Island.

HILO, HAWAII	Volcanoes National Park on the big island.
NAWILLIWILL, HAWAII	On the island of Kauai. Nice yacht club
ENSENADA, MEXICO	41 Charter Busses to San Diego end 2nd World Cruise
SAN DIEGO, CITY BALLET	Prokofiev's Romeo and Juliet. Great performance!
LONDON, ENGLAND	Three days in London, Cruise the Thames River.
DOVER, ENGLAND	Embark on Oceana Marina, bound for Barcelona.
BRUGES, BELGIUM	14th Century Flemish walled city with canals.
PARIS, (LE HARVE) FRANCE	Au Pied de Cachon, near Paris Opera, a favorite dine.
ST. MALO, FRANCE	Mont St. Michael rises from the sea at high tide.
CONCARNEAU, FRANCE	Walled city with cobblestone streets, a resort area.
LA ROCHELLE, FRANCE	Lots of yachts is this French sailors harbor.
BORDEAUX, FRANCE	Wine country to sip St. Emilion one of my favorites.
BILBAO, SPAIN	Tapas galore in the old quarter of Bilbo.
LA CARONA, SPAIN	Tower of Hercules, 2nd century lighthouse, WHS.
OPORTO, PORTUGAL	World Heritage Site, 2nd largest city in Portugal.

LISBON, PORTUGAL	Home to so many explorers with monuments to them.
SEVILLE, (CADIZ) SPAIN	Visit the Alcazar, Spain's Royal Residence.
GIBRALTAR, UK	See across to Africa from the top of the Rock.
BARCELONA, SPAIN	Las Ramblas, Stayed again at Grand Marina Hotel.
ANDORRA LA VILLA, ANDORRA	Small country in the Basque region of the Pyrenees.
MUNICH, GERMANY	Oktoberfest for two days, is an awesome celebration.
BARCELONA, SPAIN	Embark on Pullmantur Soverign bound for Nice.
TUNIS, TUNISIA	Muslim architecture abounds in this African city.
CARTHAGE, TUNISIA	Ancient city that once controlled the Mediterranean.
SIDI BOU SAID, TUNISIA	Beautiful town, white buildings, blue trim.
NAPLES, ITALY	Third largest city in Italy after Rome and Milan.
FLORENCE, ITALY	Need photo. Michelangelo's David for Ascent of Man.
NICE, FRANCE	Nice Opera House, saw Nice Ballet Mediterranean

MEMORIBLE MOMENTS

I HAVE written a lot of books on cruise ships. Typically I sit in the cat birds seat early in the morning surrounded by windows overlooking the vast ocean at the very bow of the ship, people tend to stop by and say hello.

A man named Al Noullet from Dallas, TX walked up and introduced himself and said:

"Every day you are always in the same seat, why is that?"

"So people know where to find me."

"You seem to be always working on your computer?"

"I write books and from this vantage point it is a most perfect of places to be inspired.

"It sure is."

"I am nearing the end of a 101 day trip recommended by my wife that started with a safari in Africa. The safari was something she always wanted to do."

"I see you here every day and you are always alone. Where is your wife?"

"My wife Deborah Johnson passed away 17 months ago".

"No she didn't, she has been sitting right there next to you!"

THE END

epilogue

COLCHESTER, VT	My beautiful granddaughter, Emily Davis, born to Patty and Sam.
NORTH HERO, VT	Marina International business partner take-over leaves me destitute.
NORTH HERO, VT	Business partner burns down Five Oaks home.
BURLINGTON, VT.	Settlement in my lawsuit against business partner favors plaintiff.
ST. ALBANS, VT	Business partner later killed by train, while riding back-hoe on tracks.
NORTH HERO, VT	Yacht sales have never recovered from the previous sales records.
LA JOLLA, CA	Mike meets Lori Colt while riding bike.
SAN DIEGO, CA	Shortly thereafter, Mike and Lori Colt get married.
VALLEY CENTER, CA	Mike and Lori acquire beautiful home with spectacular views.

acknowledgements

During the process of writing this book, I am thankful to the following for their advice and encouragement to publish.

Cecile Claus
Duncan Edwards
Joyce and Jack Henke
Laura Larkin Newham
Sherri Lee Books Wilfong
Joe Vasquez

And for so many mentors along the way.

Jim Ibey, Franchi Construction Co.
Henry Moritz, ITT, Federal Electric Co.
General Saleen, ITT, Federal Electric Co.
Al Cushing, System Development Corporation
Joe Kuhn, IBM
Joe King, IBM
Dr. Jack Baxter, MD
Henry J. Maloney, CLU, MONY
Dr. Lindsay A. Skinner, PhD.
Alberta and John P. Roach

John P. Roach Jr.

BROUGHT UP in Glen Rock, NJ and attained a Liberal Arts Education through study of the Classics, Philosophy and Political Science at St. Michael's College in Vermont. The author went on to take many on-campus courses in his field of interest at Seton Hall University, USC, Notre Dame University and Farleigh Dickinson University for Psychology, University of Vermont for Music and most recently Screenwriting at UCLA. Currently residing in San Diego, CA, the author has completed many screenplays and books on such diverse subjects as classical music, psychology, history, archeology, philosophy, opera, science, bigotry, politics, love and war.

"Don Quixote's message lives on!"
-Joe Vasquez

"All about kids and fathers."
-William Henry Herries

"A fascinating five generation saga."
-Sherri Lee Books, Editor

"A shower of idealism!"
-Olivia-Irene Rockman